# TEACHER'S PET PUBLICATIONS

## PUZZLE PACK
### for
### Antigone
based on the play by
Sophocles

Written by
Mary B. Collins

© 2006 Teacher's Pet Publications
All Rights Reserved

The materials in this packet are copyrighted
by Teacher's Pet Publications, Inc.

These pages may be duplicated by the purchaser
for use in the purchaser's own classroom.

Copying any of these materials and distributing them
for any other purpose is a violation of the copyright laws.

© 2006 Teacher's Pet Publications, Inc.
www.tpet.com

## INTRODUCTION
If you already own the LitPlan for this title, this Puzzle Pack will refresh your Unit Resource Materials and Vocabulary Resource Materials sections plus give you additional materials you can substitute into the tests. If you do not already have a complete LitPlan, these pages will give you some supplemental materials to use with your own plan. There are two main groups of materials: one set for unit words (such as characters' names, symbols, places, etc.) and one set for vocabulary words associated with the book.

## WORD LIST
There is a word list for both the unit words and the vocabulary words. These lists show you which words are being used in the materials and the clues or definitions being used for those words. You may want to give students a word list with clues/definitions to help them, or you may want students to only have a word list (without clues/definitions) if you want them to work a little harder. Both are available for duplication. The word lists can also be your "calling key" for the bingo games.

## FILL IN THE BLANK AND MATCHING
There are 4 each of the fill in the blank and matching worksheets for both the unit and vocabulary words. These pages can be used either as extra worksheets for students or as objective parts of a unit test. They can be done individually if students need extra help or as a whole class activity to review the material covered.

## MAGIC SQUARES
The magic squares not only reinforce the material covered but also work on reasoning and math skills. Many teachers have told us that their students really enjoy doing these!

## WORD SEARCH PUZZLES
The word search words go in all directions, as indicated on your answer keys. Two of the word search puzzles have the clues listed rather than the words. This makes the puzzle a little more difficult, but it reinforces the material better. Two word search puzzles have words only for students who find the clue puzzles too difficult.

## CROSSWORD PUZZLES
Both unit and vocabulary word sections have 4 crossword puzzles.

## BINGO CARDS
There are 32 individual bingo cards for the unit words and 32 individual bingo cards for the vocabulary words. You can use your word list as a "call list," calling the words at random and marking them off of your list as you go, or you could use the flash cards by cutting them apart and drawing the words at random from a hat (or box or whatever). To make a better review, you might ask for the definition and spelling of each word as you call it out–or you could call out the definitions and have students tell you the words they need to look for on the puzzle.

## JUGGLE LETTERS
The vocabulary juggle letter game is intended to help students learn the spellings of the words. One sheet has the definitions listed on it as an extra help for students who need it or to reinforce the definitions if you choose to do so.

## FLASH CARDS
We've included a set of vocabulary flash cards you can duplicate, cut, and fold for your students. Some teachers make a few sets for general use by the class; others make a set for each student. Some teachers duplicate them for each student and have the students cut & fold their own. You can cut out just the words and put them in a hat, have each student pick out one word and write the definition and a sentence for that word. Students then swap words and papers, with the next student adding a sentence of his own under the last one. You can have students swap as many times as you like. Each time the student will read the sentences written prior to his own and then add a sentence. You can cut out the words and definitions separately and play "I Have; Who Has?" Each student in the room draws a word and definition. The first student says, "I have (the name of the word). Who has the definition?" The student with the definition reads it then says, "I have (the name of the vocabulary word she has). Who has the definition?" The round continues until all words and definitions have been given.

**Antigone Word List**

| No. | Word | Clue/Definition |
|---|---|---|
| 1. | AESCHYLUS | Greek playwright who was defeated in the tetralogy competition by Sophocles |
| 2. | ANTIGONE | Ill-fated daughter of Oedipus; defied the king's decree |
| 3. | ANTISTROPHE | Movement of the chorus from left to right across the stage |
| 4. | BATTLE | Oedipus's 2 sons were killed in ___. |
| 5. | BIRDS | Teiresias heard these & they frightened him. |
| 6. | BURY | Creon decreed it illegal to ___ Polyneices. |
| 7. | CATHARSIS | Purification of a character's emotions; an emotional release |
| 8. | CHORAGOS | Leader of the chorus |
| 9. | CHORUS | Group that sings and comments on the actions of the characters |
| 10. | CREON | Took over as King of Thebes after the war |
| 11. | DEATH | Penalty for burying Polyneices |
| 12. | DIONYSIA | Festival honoring the Greek God of wine |
| 13. | DIONYSOS | God of wine in whose honor Greek tragedies were performed |
| 14. | EPISODE | Scene in a play |
| 15. | ETEOCLES | Oedipus's son buried with full honors |
| 16. | ETHOS | Attempt to appeal to one's sense of moral duty as persuasion |
| 17. | EURYDICE | Queen of Thebes |
| 18. | EXODUS | Last song of the play; usually contains a moral lesson |
| 19. | GOD | The fortunate man is one who has never tasted ___'s vengeance. |
| 20. | GOLD | According to Creon, all prophets love this. |
| 21. | HAIMON | Engaged to Antigone; son of Creon |
| 22. | HARMARTIA | Tragic flaw in a character's personality |
| 23. | HUBRIS | Arrogance demonstrated by a character as a result of his/her pride or passion |
| 24. | ISMENE | Refused to help her sister bury Polyneices |
| 25. | LANGUAGE | One of man's accomplishments: he created ___ |
| 26. | LOGOS | Attempt to use reason as a means of persuasion |
| 27. | LOVE | Even the pure Immortals cannot escape it. |
| 28. | MAN | ___ is the most wonderful of all the world's wonders. |
| 29. | ODES | Songs that comment on the action of the play or its characters |
| 30. | OEDIPUS | Killed his father & married his mother; father of Antigone |
| 31. | PAEAN | Prayer of thanksgiving to Dionysos at the end of the play |
| 32. | PARADOS | Opening song as the chorus makes its entrance |
| 33. | PATHOS | Attempt to use emotion as a means of persuasion |
| 34. | POLYNEICES | Considered a traitor to Thebes; his body was left to rot |
| 35. | PROLOGUE | Introduces the main characters at the beginning of the play |
| 36. | REASON | God's crowning gift to man, according to Haimon |
| 37. | SATYR | Play that comically portrayed mythological stories or poked fun at politics |
| 38. | SEAS | One of man's accomplishments: he conquered the ___ |
| 39. | SISTERS | Relationship between Antigone and Ismene |
| 40. | SOPHOCLES | Author of the play Antigone |
| 41. | SOUL | When his body was buried, Polyneices's ___ could move to the Underworld. |
| 42. | STROPHE | Movement of the chorus from right to left across the stage |
| 43. | TEIRESIAS | Blind prophet |
| 44. | TETRAOLOGY | Collection of plays submitted in the Dionysia competition |
| 45. | THEBES | It has seven gates in a yawning ring. |
| 46. | THESPIS | Considered to be the Father of Greek Theater |
| 47. | TRAGEDY | Serious play in which the main character suffers from a flaw |

## Antigone Word List

| No. | Word | Clue/Definition |
|---|---|---|
| 48. | ZEUS | Those who anger him will suffer his wrath. |

Antigone Fill In The Blanks 1

_____ 1. ___ is the most wonderful of all the world's wonders.

_____ 2. When his body was buried, Polyneices's ___ could move to the Underworld.

_____ 3. God's crowning gift to man, according to Haimon

_____ 4. Greek playwright who was defeated in the tetralogy competition by Sophocles

_____ 5. Oedipus's 2 sons were killed in ___.

_____ 6. One of man's accomplishments: he conquered the ___

_____ 7. Festival honoring the Greek God of wine

_____ 8. Songs that comment on the action of the play or its characters

_____ 9. Movement of the chorus from left to right across the stage

_____ 10. Arrogance demonstrated by a character as a result of his/her pride or passion

_____ 11. Attempt to appeal to one's sense of moral duty as persuasion

_____ 12. Considered to be the Father of Greek Theater

_____ 13. Those who anger him will suffer his wrath.

_____ 14. Took over as King of Thebes after the war

_____ 15. Oedipus's son buried with full honors

_____ 16. According to Creon, all prophets love this.

_____ 17. Leader of the chorus

_____ 18. Tragic flaw in a character's personality

_____ 19. Considered a traitor to Thebes; his body was left to rot

_____ 20. Blind prophet

Antigone Fill In The Blanks 1 Answer Key

| | |
|---|---|
| MAN | 1. ___ is the most wonderful of all the world's wonders. |
| SOUL | 2. When his body was buried, Polyneices's ___ could move to the Underworld. |
| REASON | 3. God's crowning gift to man, according to Haimon |
| AESCHYLUS | 4. Greek playwright who was defeated in the tetralogy competition by Sophocles |
| BATTLE | 5. Oedipus's 2 sons were killed in ___. |
| SEAS | 6. One of man's accomplishments: he conquered the ___ |
| DIONYSIA | 7. Festival honoring the Greek God of wine |
| ODES | 8. Songs that comment on the action of the play or its characters |
| ANTISTROPHE | 9. Movement of the chorus from left to right across the stage |
| HUBRIS | 10. Arrogance demonstrated by a character as a result of his/her pride or passion |
| ETHOS | 11. Attempt to appeal to one's sense of moral duty as persuasion |
| THESPIS | 12. Considered to be the Father of Greek Theater |
| ZEUS | 13. Those who anger him will suffer his wrath. |
| CREON | 14. Took over as King of Thebes after the war |
| ETEOCLES | 15. Oedipus's son buried with full honors |
| GOLD | 16. According to Creon, all prophets love this. |
| CHORAGOS | 17. Leader of the chorus |
| HARMARTIA | 18. Tragic flaw in a character's personality |
| POLYNEICES | 19. Considered a traitor to Thebes; his body was left to rot |
| TEIRESIAS | 20. Blind prophet |

Antigone Fill In The Blanks 2

_____ 1. It has seven gates in a yawning ring.
_____ 2. According to Creon, all prophets love this.
_____ 3. Considered a traitor to Thebes; his body was left to rot
_____ 4. Blind prophet
_____ 5. Considered to be the Father of Greek Theater
_____ 6. Opening song as the chorus makes its entrance
_____ 7. Engaged to Antigone; son of Creon
_____ 8. Attempt to use emotion as a means of persuasion
_____ 9. Festival honoring the Greek God of wine
_____ 10. Prayer of thanksgiving to Dionysos at the end of the play
_____ 11. Those who anger him will suffer his wrath.
_____ 12. Introduces the main characters at the beginning of the play
_____ 13. Leader of the chorus
_____ 14. ___ is the most wonderful of all the world's wonders.
_____ 15. Play that comically portrayed mythological stories or poked fun at politics
_____ 16. Serious play in which the main character suffers from a flaw
_____ 17. Refused to help her sister bury Polyneices
_____ 18. Scene in a play
_____ 19. One of man's accomplishments: he created ___
_____ 20. Movement of the chorus from left to right across the stage

Antigone Fill In The Blanks 2 Answer Key

| | |
|---|---|
| THEBES | 1. It has seven gates in a yawning ring. |
| GOLD | 2. According to Creon, all prophets love this. |
| POLYNEICES | 3. Considered a traitor to Thebes; his body was left to rot |
| TEIRESIAS | 4. Blind prophet |
| THESPIS | 5. Considered to be the Father of Greek Theater |
| PARADOS | 6. Opening song as the chorus makes its entrance |
| HAIMON | 7. Engaged to Antigone; son of Creon |
| PATHOS | 8. Attempt to use emotion as a means of persuasion |
| DIONYSIA | 9. Festival honoring the Greek God of wine |
| PAEAN | 10. Prayer of thanksgiving to Dionysos at the end of the play |
| ZEUS | 11. Those who anger him will suffer his wrath. |
| PROLOGUE | 12. Introduces the main characters at the beginning of the play |
| CHORAGOS | 13. Leader of the chorus |
| MAN | 14. ___ is the most wonderful of all the world's wonders. |
| SATYR | 15. Play that comically portrayed mythological stories or poked fun at politics |
| TRAGEDY | 16. Serious play in which the main character suffers from a flaw |
| ISMENE | 17. Refused to help her sister bury Polyneices |
| EPISODE | 18. Scene in a play |
| LANGUAGE | 19. One of man's accomplishments: he created ___ |
| ANTISTROPHE | 20. Movement of the chorus from left to right across the stage |

Antigone Fill In The Blanks 3

_____  1. Scene in a play

_____  2. Relationship between Antigone and Ismene

_____  3. Collection of plays submitted in the Dionysia competition

_____  4. It has seven gates in a yawning ring.

_____  5. God of wine in whose honor Greek tragedies were performed

_____  6. Arrogance demonstrated by a character as a result of his/her pride or passion

_____  7. Attempt to appeal to one's sense of moral duty as persuasion

_____  8. Attempt to use emotion as a means of persuasion

_____  9. Creon decreed it illegal to ___ Polyneices.

_____  10. Group that sings and comments on the actions of the characters

_____  11. Play that comically portrayed mythological stories or poked fun at politics

_____  12. Queen of Thebes

_____  13. Tragic flaw in a character's personality

_____  14. Author of the play Antigone

_____  15. According to Creon, all prophets love this.

_____  16. Penalty for burying Polyneices

_____  17. When his body was buried, Polyneices's ___ could move to the Underworld.

_____  18. ___ is the most wonderful of all the world's wonders.

_____  19. Movement of the chorus from left to right across the stage

_____  20. Blind prophet

Antigone Fill In The Blanks 3 Answer Key

| | |
|---|---|
| EPISODE | 1. Scene in a play |
| SISTERS | 2. Relationship between Antigone and Ismene |
| TETRAOLOGY | 3. Collection of plays submitted in the Dionysia competition |
| THEBES | 4. It has seven gates in a yawning ring. |
| DIONYSOS | 5. God of wine in whose honor Greek tragedies were performed |
| HUBRIS | 6. Arrogance demonstrated by a character as a result of his/her pride or passion |
| ETHOS | 7. Attempt to appeal to one's sense of moral duty as persuasion |
| PATHOS | 8. Attempt to use emotion as a means of persuasion |
| BURY | 9. Creon decreed it illegal to ___ Polyneices. |
| CHORUS | 10. Group that sings and comments on the actions of the characters |
| SATYR | 11. Play that comically portrayed mythological stories or poked fun at politics |
| EURYDICE | 12. Queen of Thebes |
| HARMARTIA | 13. Tragic flaw in a character's personality |
| SOPHOCLES | 14. Author of the play Antigone |
| GOLD | 15. According to Creon, all prophets love this. |
| DEATH | 16. Penalty for burying Polyneices |
| SOUL | 17. When his body was buried, Polyneices's ___ could move to the Underworld. |
| MAN | 18. ___ is the most wonderful of all the world's wonders. |
| ANTISTROPHE | 19. Movement of the chorus from left to right across the stage |
| TEIRESIAS | 20. Blind prophet |

Antigone Fill In The Blanks 4

_____   1. Refused to help her sister bury Polyneices

_____   2. Relationship between Antigone and Ismene

_____   3. According to Creon, all prophets love this.

_____   4. Took over as King of Thebes after the war

_____   5. Considered a traitor to Thebes; his body was left to rot

_____   6. Serious play in which the main character suffers from a flaw

_____   7. Attempt to use reason as a means of persuasion

_____   8. Opening song as the chorus makes its entrance

_____   9. Killed his father & married his mother; father of Antigone

_____   10. Creon decreed it illegal to ___ Polyneices.

_____   11. Queen of Thebes

_____   12. Engaged to Antigone; son of Creon

_____   13. Oedipus's son buried with full honors

_____   14. Penalty for burying Polyneices

_____   15. It has seven gates in a yawning ring.

_____   16. Greek playwright who was defeated in the tetralogy competition by Sophocles

_____   17. ___ is the most wonderful of all the world's wonders.

_____   18. Even the pure Immortals cannot escape it.

_____   19. When his body was buried, Polyneices's ___ could move to the Underworld.

_____   20. Scene in a play

Antigone Fill In The Blanks 4 Answer Key

| | |
|---|---|
| ISMENE | 1. Refused to help her sister bury Polyneices |
| SISTERS | 2. Relationship between Antigone and Ismene |
| GOLD | 3. According to Creon, all prophets love this. |
| CREON | 4. Took over as King of Thebes after the war |
| POLYNEICES | 5. Considered a traitor to Thebes; his body was left to rot |
| TRAGEDY | 6. Serious play in which the main character suffers from a flaw |
| LOGOS | 7. Attempt to use reason as a means of persuasion |
| PARADOS | 8. Opening song as the chorus makes its entrance |
| OEDIPUS | 9. Killed his father & married his mother; father of Antigone |
| BURY | 10. Creon decreed it illegal to ___ Polyneices. |
| EURYDICE | 11. Queen of Thebes |
| HAIMON | 12. Engaged to Antigone; son of Creon |
| ETEOCLES | 13. Oedipus's son buried with full honors |
| DEATH | 14. Penalty for burying Polyneices |
| THEBES | 15. It has seven gates in a yawning ring. |
| AESCHYLUS | 16. Greek playwright who was defeated in the tetralogy competition by Sophocles |
| MAN | 17. ___ is the most wonderful of all the world's wonders. |
| LOVE | 18. Even the pure Immortals cannot escape it. |
| SOUL | 19. When his body was buried, Polyneices's ___ could move to the Underworld. |
| EPISODE | 20. Scene in a play |

Antigone Matching 1

___ 1. EURYDICE
___ 2. POLYNEICES
___ 3. EXODUS
___ 4. HAIMON
___ 5. LOGOS
___ 6. CHORUS
___ 7. SOPHOCLES
___ 8. OEDIPUS
___ 9. BURY
___ 10. ANTISTROPHE
___ 11. ETHOS
___ 12. ODES
___ 13. EPISODE
___ 14. TETRAOLOGY
___ 15. STROPHE
___ 16. ETEOCLES
___ 17. BATTLE
___ 18. MAN
___ 19. AESCHYLUS
___ 20. SATYR
___ 21. THESPIS
___ 22. THEBES
___ 23. ZEUS
___ 24. DEATH
___ 25. BIRDS

A. Greek playwright who was defeated in the tetralogy competition by Sophocles
B. Play that comically portrayed mythological stories or poked fun at politics
C. It has seven gates in a yawning ring.
D. Last song of the play; usually contains a moral lesson
E. ___ is the most wonderful of all the world's wonders.
F. Scene in a play
G. Those who anger him will suffer his wrath.
H. Oedipus's 2 sons were killed in ___.
I. Songs that comment on the action of the play or its characters
J. Author of the play Antigone
K. Creon decreed it illegal to ___ Polyneices.
L. Oedipus's son buried with full honors
M. Killed his father & married his mother; father of Antigone
N. Group that sings and comments on the actions of the characters
O. Attempt to use reason as a means of persuasion
P. Attempt to appeal to one's sense of moral duty as persuasion
Q. Collection of plays submitted in the Dionysia competition
R. Teiresias heard these & they frightened him.
S. Considered a traitor to Thebes; his body was left to rot
T. Engaged to Antigone; son of Creon
U. Movement of the chorus from left to right across the stage
V. Queen of Thebes
W. Considered to be the Father of Greek Theater
X. Penalty for burying Polyneices
Y. Movement of the chorus from right to left across the stage

Antigone Matching 1 Answer Key

| | | |
|---|---|---|
| V - 1. EURYDICE | A. | Greek playwright who was defeated in the tetralogy competition by Sophocles |
| S - 2. POLYNEICES | B. | Play that comically portrayed mythological stories or poked fun at politics |
| D - 3. EXODUS | C. | It has seven gates in a yawning ring. |
| T - 4. HAIMON | D. | Last song of the play; usually contains a moral lesson |
| O - 5. LOGOS | E. | ___ is the most wonderful of all the world's wonders. |
| N - 6. CHORUS | F. | Scene in a play |
| J - 7. SOPHOCLES | G. | Those who anger him will suffer his wrath. |
| M - 8. OEDIPUS | H. | Oedipus's 2 sons were killed in ___. |
| K - 9. BURY | I. | Songs that comment on the action of the play or its characters |
| U -10. ANTISTROPHE | J. | Author of the play Antigone |
| P -11. ETHOS | K. | Creon decreed it illegal to ___ Polyneices. |
| I - 12. ODES | L. | Oedipus's son buried with full honors |
| F - 13. EPISODE | M. | Killed his father & married his mother; father of Antigone |
| Q -14. TETRAOLOGY | N. | Group that sings and comments on the actions of the characters |
| Y -15. STROPHE | O. | Attempt to use reason as a means of persuasion |
| L - 16. ETEOCLES | P. | Attempt to appeal to one's sense of moral duty as persuasion |
| H -17. BATTLE | Q. | Collection of plays submitted in the Dionysia competition |
| E - 18. MAN | R. | Teiresias heard these & they frightened him. |
| A - 19. AESCHYLUS | S. | Considered a traitor to Thebes; his body was left to rot |
| B -20. SATYR | T. | Engaged to Antigone; son of Creon |
| W -21. THESPIS | U. | Movement of the chorus from left to right across the stage |
| C -22. THEBES | V. | Queen of Thebes |
| G -23. ZEUS | W. | Considered to be the Father of Greek Theater |
| X -24. DEATH | X. | Penalty for burying Polyneices |
| R -25. BIRDS | Y. | Movement of the chorus from right to left across the stage |

Antigone Matching 2

___ 1. AESCHYLUS         A. Collection of plays submitted in the Dionysia competition
___ 2. HUBRIS            B. Those who anger him will suffer his wrath.
___ 3. CHORAGOS          C. Introduces the main characters at the beginning of the play
___ 4. ETHOS             D. Arrogance demonstrated by a character as a result of his/her pride or passion
___ 5. MAN               E. Creon decreed it illegal to ___ Polyneices.
___ 6. ZEUS              F. Took over as King of Thebes after the war
___ 7. REASON            G. ___ is the most wonderful of all the world's wonders.
___ 8. CREON             H. Even the pure Immortals cannot escape it.
___ 9. EURYDICE          I. Scene in a play
___10. TETRAOLOGY        J. God's crowning gift to man, according to Haimon
___11. DEATH             K. Festival honoring the Greek God of wine
___12. DIONYSIA          L. Teiresias heard these & they frightened him.
___13. LOVE              M. Songs that comment on the action of the play or its characters
___14. TRAGEDY           N. Refused to help her sister bury Polyneices
___15. GOD               O. Leader of the chorus
___16. ISMENE            P. Penalty for burying Polyneices
___17. CATHARSIS         Q. The fortunate man is one who has never tasted ___'s vengeance.
___18. ODES              R. Greek playwright who was defeated in the tetralogy competition by Sophocles
___19. PROLOGUE          S. Queen of Thebes
___20. BIRDS             T. Attempt to appeal to one's sense of moral duty as persuasion
___21. OEDIPUS           U. Serious play in which the main character suffers from a flaw
___22. ANTISTROPHE       V. Engaged to Antigone; son of Creon
___23. BURY              W. Killed his father & married his mother; father of Antigone
___24. EPISODE           X. Movement of the chorus from left to right across the stage
___25. HAIMON            Y. Purification of a character's emotions; an emotional release

Antigone Matching 2 Answer Key

| | | |
|---|---|---|
| R - 1. | AESCHYLUS | A. Collection of plays submitted in the Dionysia competition |
| D - 2. | HUBRIS | B. Those who anger him will suffer his wrath. |
| O - 3. | CHORAGOS | C. Introduces the main characters at the beginning of the play |
| T - 4. | ETHOS | D. Arrogance demonstrated by a character as a result of his/her pride or passion |
| G - 5. | MAN | E. Creon decreed it illegal to ___ Polyneices. |
| B - 6. | ZEUS | F. Took over as King of Thebes after the war |
| J - 7. | REASON | G. ___ is the most wonderful of all the world's wonders. |
| F - 8. | CREON | H. Even the pure Immortals cannot escape it. |
| S - 9. | EURYDICE | I. Scene in a play |
| A -10. | TETRAOLOGY | J. God's crowning gift to man, according to Haimon |
| P -11. | DEATH | K. Festival honoring the Greek God of wine |
| K -12. | DIONYSIA | L. Teiresias heard these & they frightened him. |
| H -13. | LOVE | M. Songs that comment on the action of the play or its characters |
| U -14. | TRAGEDY | N. Refused to help her sister bury Polyneices |
| Q -15. | GOD | O. Leader of the chorus |
| N -16. | ISMENE | P. Penalty for burying Polyneices |
| Y -17. | CATHARSIS | Q. The fortunate man is one who has never tasted ___'s vengeance. |
| M -18. | ODES | R. Greek playwright who was defeated in the tetralogy competition by Sophocles |
| C -19. | PROLOGUE | S. Queen of Thebes |
| L -20. | BIRDS | T. Attempt to appeal to one's sense of moral duty as persuasion |
| W -21. | OEDIPUS | U. Serious play in which the main character suffers from a flaw |
| X -22. | ANTISTROPHE | V. Engaged to Antigone; son of Creon |
| E -23. | BURY | W. Killed his father & married his mother; father of Antigone |
| I - 24. | EPISODE | X. Movement of the chorus from left to right across the stage |
| V -25. | HAIMON | Y. Purification of a character's emotions; an emotional release |

Antigone Matching 3

___ 1. CATHARSIS          A. Teiresias heard these & they frightened him.
___ 2. ODES               B. When his body was buried, Polyneices's ___ could move to the Underworld.
___ 3. PATHOS             C. Queen of Thebes
___ 4. DIONYSIA           D. It has seven gates in a yawning ring.
___ 5. HAIMON             E. Festival honoring the Greek God of wine
___ 6. SOUL               F. Attempt to use emotion as a means of persuasion
___ 7. EXODUS             G. Penalty for burying Polyneices
___ 8. BURY               H. Attempt to appeal to one's sense of moral duty as persuasion
___ 9. BIRDS              I. Oedipus's son buried with full honors
___10. STROPHE            J. Purification of a character's emotions; an emotional release
___11. PARADOS            K. Opening song as the chorus makes its entrance
___12. EURYDICE           L. Songs that comment on the action of the play or its characters
___13. ETEOCLES           M. God's crowning gift to man, according to Haimon
___14. TRAGEDY            N. Last song of the play; usually contains a moral lesson
___15. TEIRESIAS          O. Serious play in which the main character suffers from a flaw
___16. PROLOGUE           P. Oedipus's 2 sons were killed in ___.
___17. HUBRIS             Q. Engaged to Antigone; son of Creon
___18. ETHOS              R. Blind prophet
___19. REASON             S. Scene in a play
___20. HARMARTIA          T. Introduces the main characters at the beginning of the play
___21. DEATH              U. Movement of the chorus from right to left across the stage
___22. BATTLE             V. Creon decreed it illegal to ___ Polyneices.
___23. EPISODE            W. Tragic flaw in a character's personality
___24. THEBES             X. Arrogance demonstrated by a character as a result of his/her pride or passion
___25. CREON              Y. Took over as King of Thebes after the war

Antigone Matching 3 Answer Key

J - 1. CATHARSIS          A. Teiresias heard these & they frightened him.
L - 2. ODES               B. When his body was buried, Polyneices's ___ could move to the Underworld.
F - 3. PATHOS             C. Queen of Thebes
E - 4. DIONYSIA           D. It has seven gates in a yawning ring.
Q - 5. HAIMON             E. Festival honoring the Greek God of wine
B - 6. SOUL               F. Attempt to use emotion as a means of persuasion
N - 7. EXODUS             G. Penalty for burying Polyneices
V - 8. BURY               H. Attempt to appeal to one's sense of moral duty as persuasion
A - 9. BIRDS              I. Oedipus's son buried with full honors
U -10. STROPHE            J. Purification of a character's emotions; an emotional release
K -11. PARADOS            K. Opening song as the chorus makes its entrance
C -12. EURYDICE           L. Songs that comment on the action of the play or its characters
I -13. ETEOCLES           M. God's crowning gift to man, according to Haimon
O -14. TRAGEDY            N. Last song of the play; usually contains a moral lesson
R -15. TEIRESIAS          O. Serious play in which the main character suffers from a flaw
T -16. PROLOGUE           P. Oedipus's 2 sons were killed in ___.
X -17. HUBRIS             Q. Engaged to Antigone; son of Creon
H -18. ETHOS              R. Blind prophet
M -19. REASON             S. Scene in a play
W -20. HARMARTIA          T. Introduces the main characters at the beginning of the play
G -21. DEATH              U. Movement of the chorus from right to left across the stage
P -22. BATTLE             V. Creon decreed it illegal to ___ Polyneices.
S -23. EPISODE            W. Tragic flaw in a character's personality
D -24. THEBES             X. Arrogance demonstrated by a character as a result of his/her pride or passion
Y -25. CREON              Y. Took over as King of Thebes after the war

Antigone Matching 4

___ 1. SEAS  A. Took over as King of Thebes after the war
___ 2. PROLOGUE  B. Those who anger him will suffer his wrath.
___ 3. EPISODE  C. ___ is the most wonderful of all the world's wonders.
___ 4. CHORUS  D. Purification of a character's emotions; an emotional release
___ 5. ETHOS  E. Attempt to appeal to one's sense of moral duty as persuasion
___ 6. ODES  F. Festival honoring the Greek God of wine
___ 7. ZEUS  G. Scene in a play
___ 8. CATHARSIS  H. Teiresias heard these & they frightened him.
___ 9. PARADOS  I. Greek playwright who was defeated in the tetralogy competition by Sophocles
___ 10. ISMENE  J. Group that sings and comments on the actions of the characters
___ 11. GOD  K. God of wine in whose honor Greek tragedies were performed
___ 12. AESCHYLUS  L. Blind prophet
___ 13. THEBES  M. Refused to help her sister bury Polyneices
___ 14. CREON  N. According to Creon, all prophets love this.
___ 15. BATTLE  O. Relationship between Antigone and Ismene
___ 16. DIONYSIA  P. Tragic flaw in a character's personality
___ 17. BIRDS  Q. Collection of plays submitted in the Dionysia competition
___ 18. MAN  R. Opening song as the chorus makes its entrance
___ 19. LOGOS  S. Oedipus's 2 sons were killed in ___.
___ 20. TETRAOLOGY  T. The fortunate man is one who has never tasted ___'s vengeance.
___ 21. SISTERS  U. Introduces the main characters at the beginning of the play
___ 22. GOLD  V. It has seven gates in a yawning ring.
___ 23. HARMARTIA  W. Songs that comment on the action of the play or its characters
___ 24. TEIRESIAS  X. One of man's accomplishments: he conquered the ___
___ 25. DIONYSOS  Y. Attempt to use reason as a means of persuasion

Antigone Matching 4 Answer Key

| | | |
|---|---|---|
| X - 1. | SEAS | A. Took over as King of Thebes after the war |
| U - 2. | PROLOGUE | B. Those who anger him will suffer his wrath. |
| G - 3. | EPISODE | C. ___ is the most wonderful of all the world's wonders. |
| J - 4. | CHORUS | D. Purification of a character's emotions; an emotional release |
| E - 5. | ETHOS | E. Attempt to appeal to one's sense of moral duty as persuasion |
| W - 6. | ODES | F. Festival honoring the Greek God of wine |
| B - 7. | ZEUS | G. Scene in a play |
| D - 8. | CATHARSIS | H. Teiresias heard these & they frightened him. |
| R - 9. | PARADOS | I. Greek playwright who was defeated in the tetralogy competition by Sophocles |
| M - 10. | ISMENE | J. Group that sings and comments on the actions of the characters |
| T - 11. | GOD | K. God of wine in whose honor Greek tragedies were performed |
| I - 12. | AESCHYLUS | L. Blind prophet |
| V - 13. | THEBES | M. Refused to help her sister bury Polyneices |
| A - 14. | CREON | N. According to Creon, all prophets love this. |
| S - 15. | BATTLE | O. Relationship between Antigone and Ismene |
| F - 16. | DIONYSIA | P. Tragic flaw in a character's personality |
| H - 17. | BIRDS | Q. Collection of plays submitted in the Dionysia competition |
| C - 18. | MAN | R. Opening song as the chorus makes its entrance |
| Y - 19. | LOGOS | S. Oedipus's 2 sons were killed in ___. |
| Q - 20. | TETRAOLOGY | T. The fortunate man is one who has never tasted ___'s vengeance. |
| O - 21. | SISTERS | U. Introduces the main characters at the beginning of the play |
| N - 22. | GOLD | V. It has seven gates in a yawning ring. |
| P - 23. | HARMARTIA | W. Songs that comment on the action of the play or its characters |
| L - 24. | TEIRESIAS | X. One of man's accomplishments: he conquered the ___ |
| K - 25. | DIONYSOS | Y. Attempt to use reason as a means of persuasion |

Antigone Magic Squares 1

Match the definition with the vocabulary word. Put your answers in the magic squares below. When your answers are correct, all columns and rows will add to the same number.

A. LOGOS  
B. ETHOS  
C. REASON  
D. PROLOGUE  
E. TEIRESIAS  
F. SOUL  
G. PARADOS  
H. SEAS  
I. SOPHOCLES  
J. DIONYSOS  
K. ANTIGONE  
L. DEATH  
M. AESCHYLUS  
N. BATTLE  
O. CHORAGOS  
P. TETRAOLOGY  

1. When his body was buried, Polyneices's ___ could move to the Underworld.
2. Author of the play Antigone
3. Leader of the chorus
4. Introduces the main characters at the beginning of the play
5. Greek playwright who was defeated in the tetralogy competition by Sophocles
6. Attempt to appeal to one's sense of moral duty as persuasion
7. One of man's accomplishments: he conquered the ___
8. Ill-fated daughter of Oedipus; defied the king's decree
9. God's crowning gift to man, according to Haimon
10. Collection of plays submitted in the Dionysia competition
11. God of wine in whose honor Greek tragedies were performed
12. Blind prophet
13. Penalty for burying Polyneices
14. Opening song as the chorus makes its entrance
15. Attempt to use reason as a means of persuasion
16. Oedipus's 2 sons were killed in ___.

| A= | B= | C= | D= |
| --- | --- | --- | --- |
| E= | F= | G= | H= |
| I= | J= | K= | L= |
| M= | N= | O= | P= |

Antigone Magic Squares 1 Answer Key

Match the definition with the vocabulary word. Put your answers in the magic squares below. When your answers are correct, all columns and rows will add to the same number.

A. LOGOS
B. ETHOS
C. REASON
D. PROLOGUE
E. TEIRESIAS
F. SOUL
G. PARADOS
H. SEAS
I. SOPHOCLES
J. DIONYSOS
K. ANTIGONE
L. DEATH
M. AESCHYLUS
N. BATTLE
O. CHORAGOS
P. TETRAOLOGY

1. When his body was buried, Polyneices's ___ could move to the Underworld.
2. Author of the play Antigone
3. Leader of the chorus
4. Introduces the main characters at the beginning of the play
5. Greek playwright who was defeated in the tetralogy competition by Sophocles
6. Attempt to appeal to one's sense of moral duty as persuasion
7. One of man's accomplishments: he conquered the ___
8. Ill-fated daughter of Oedipus; defied the king's decree
9. God's crowning gift to man, according to Haimon
10. Collection of plays submitted in the Dionysia competition
11. God of wine in whose honor Greek tragedies were performed
12. Blind prophet
13. Penalty for burying Polyneices
14. Opening song as the chorus makes its entrance
15. Attempt to use reason as a means of persuasion
16. Oedipus's 2 sons were killed in ___.

| A=15 | B=6 | C=9 | D=4 |
| --- | --- | --- | --- |
| E=12 | F=1 | G=14 | H=7 |
| I=2 | J=11 | K=8 | L=13 |
| M=5 | N=16 | O=3 | P=10 |

Antigone Magic Squares 2

Match the definition with the vocabulary word. Put your answers in the magic squares below. When your answers are correct, all columns and rows will add to the same number.

A. CATHARSIS  E. LOGOS  I. ANTISTROPHE  M. SOPHOCLES
B. ANTIGONE  F. HAIMON  J. PATHOS  N. SATYR
C. SOUL  G. BURY  K. HARMARTIA  O. PROLOGUE
D. ETHOS  H. EURYDICE  L. THEBES  P. ZEUS

1. Queen of Thebes
2. Author of the play Antigone
3. Ill-fated daughter of Oedipus; defied the king's decree
4. Tragic flaw in a character's personality
5. Attempt to use emotion as a means of persuasion
6. When his body was buried, Polyneices's ___ could move to the Underworld.
7. Those who anger him will suffer his wrath.
8. Attempt to use reason as a means of persuasion
9. Introduces the main characters at the beginning of the play
10. Engaged to Antigone; son of Creon
11. Movement of the chorus from left to right across the stage
12. Attempt to appeal to one's sense of moral duty as persuasion
13. Purification of a character's emotions; an emotional release
14. It has seven gates in a yawning ring.
15. Creon decreed it illegal to ___ Polyneices.
16. Play that comically portrayed mythological stories or poked fun at politics politics

| A= | B= | C= | D= |
| E= | F= | G= | H= |
| I= | J= | K= | L= |
| M= | N= | O= | P= |

# Antigone Magic Squares 2 Answer Key

Match the definition with the vocabulary word. Put your answers in the magic squares below. When your answers are correct, all columns and rows will add to the same number.

A. CATHARSIS
B. ANTIGONE
C. SOUL
D. ETHOS
E. LOGOS
F. HAIMON
G. BURY
H. EURYDICE
I. ANTISTROPHE
J. PATHOS
K. HARMARTIA
L. THEBES
M. SOPHOCLES
N. SATYR
O. PROLOGUE
P. ZEUS

1. Queen of Thebes
2. Author of the play Antigone
3. Ill-fated daughter of Oedipus; defied the king's decree
4. Tragic flaw in a character's personality
5. Attempt to use emotion as a means of persuasion
6. When his body was buried, Polyneices's ___ could move to the Underworld.
7. Those who anger him will suffer his wrath.
8. Attempt to use reason as a means of persuasion
9. Introduces the main characters at the beginning of the play
10. Engaged to Antigone; son of Creon
11. Movement of the chorus from left to right across the stage
12. Attempt to appeal to one's sense of moral duty as persuasion
13. Purification of a character's emotions; an emotional release
14. It has seven gates in a yawning ring.
15. Creon decreed it illegal to ___ Polyneices.
16. Play that comically portrayed mythological stories or poked fun at politics politics

| A=13 | B=3 | C=6 | D=12 |
|---|---|---|---|
| E=8 | F=10 | G=15 | H=1 |
| I=11 | J=5 | K=4 | L=14 |
| M=2 | N=16 | O=9 | P=7 |

Antigone Magic Squares 3

Match the definition with the vocabulary word. Put your answers in the magic squares below. When your answers are correct, all columns and rows will add to the same number.

A. DIONYSOS	E. ISMENE	I. PAEAN	M. HAIMON
B. SATYR	F. BURY	J. CHORAGOS	N. PATHOS
C. ETEOCLES	G. DEATH	K. BATTLE	O. HUBRIS
D. GOD	H. TRAGEDY	L. CATHARSIS	P. ZEUS

1. God of wine in whose honor Greek tragedies were performed
2. Attempt to use emotion as a means of persuasion
3. Leader of the chorus
4. Refused to help her sister bury Polyneices
5. Penalty for burying Polyneices
6. Purification of a character's emotions; an emotional release
7. Those who anger him will suffer his wrath.
8. Oedipus's son buried with full honors
9. Arrogance demonstrated by a character as a result of his/her pride or passion
10. The fortunate man is one who has never tasted ___'s vengeance.
11. Serious play in which the main character suffers from a flaw
12. Oedipus's 2 sons were killed in ___.
13. Prayer of thanksgiving to Dionysos at the end of the play
14. Creon decreed it illegal to ___ Polyneices.
15. Play that comically portrayed mythological stories or poked fun at politics
16. Engaged to Antigone; son of Creon

| A= 1 | B= 15 | C= 8 | D= 10 |
| --- | --- | --- | --- |
| E= 4 | F= 14 | G= 5 | H= 11 |
| I= 13 | J= 3 | K= 12 | L= 6 |
| M= 16 | N= 2 | O= 9 | P= 7 |

Antigone Magic Squares 3 Answer Key

Match the definition with the vocabulary word. Put your answers in the magic squares below. When your answers are correct, all columns and rows will add to the same number.

A. DIONYSOS
B. SATYR
C. ETEOCLES
D. GOD
E. ISMENE
F. BURY
G. DEATH
H. TRAGEDY
I. PAEAN
J. CHORAGOS
K. BATTLE
L. CATHARSIS
M. HAIMON
N. PATHOS
O. HUBRIS
P. ZEUS

1. God of wine in whose honor Greek tragedies were performed
2. Attempt to use emotion as a means of persuasion
3. Leader of the chorus
4. Refused to help her sister bury Polyneices
5. Penalty for burying Polyneices
6. Purification of a character's emotions; an emotional release
7. Those who anger him will suffer his wrath.
8. Oedipus's son buried with full honors
9. Arrogance demonstrated by a character as a result of his/her pride or passion
10. The fortunate man is one who has never tasted ___'s vengeance.
11. Serious play in which the main character suffers from a flaw
12. Oedipus's 2 sons were killed in ___.
13. Prayer of thanksgiving to Dionysos at the end of the play
14. Creon decreed it illegal to ___ Polyneices.
15. Play that comically portrayed mythological stories or poked fun at politics
16. Engaged to Antigone; son of Creon

| A=1 | B=15 | C=8 | D=10 |
|---|---|---|---|
| E=4 | F=14 | G=5 | H=11 |
| I=13 | J=3 | K=12 | L=6 |
| M=16 | N=2 | O=9 | P=7 |

Antigone Magic Squares 4

Match the definition with the vocabulary word. Put your answers in the magic squares below. When your answers are correct, all columns and rows will add to the same number.

A. LOVE        E. SEAS         I. BIRDS         M. BURY
B. EXODUS      F. CHORUS       J. GOLD          N. REASON
C. SATYR       G. CATHARSIS    K. TETRAOLOGY    O. HAIMON
D. PROLOGUE    H. GOD          L. ZEUS          P. STROPHE

1. The fortunate man is one who has never tasted ___'s vengeance.
2. Even the pure Immortals cannot escape it.
3. Last song of the play; usually contains a moral lesson
4. Purification of a character's emotions; an emotional release
5. According to Creon, all prophets love this.
6. Engaged to Antigone; son of Creon
7. Movement of the chorus from right to left across the stage
8. Teiresias heard these & they frightened him.
9. Collection of plays submitted in the Dionysia competition
10. God's crowning gift to man, according to Haimon
11. Creon decreed it illegal to ___ Polyneices.
12. Those who anger him will suffer his wrath.
13. One of man's accomplishments: he conquered the ___
14. Introduces the main characters at the beginning of the play
15. Play that comically portrayed mythological stories or poked fun at politics
16. Group that sings and comments on the actions of the characters

| A= | B= | C= | D= |
|---|---|---|---|
| E= | F= | G= | H= |
| I= | J= | K= | L= |
| M= | N= | O= | P= |

Antigone Magic Squares 4 Answer Key

Match the definition with the vocabulary word. Put your answers in the magic squares below. When your answers are correct, all columns and rows will add to the same number.

A. LOVE
B. EXODUS
C. SATYR
D. PROLOGUE
E. SEAS
F. CHORUS
G. CATHARSIS
H. GOD
I. BIRDS
J. GOLD
K. TETRAOLOGY
L. ZEUS
M. BURY
N. REASON
O. HAIMON
P. STROPHE

1. The fortunate man is one who has never tasted ___'s vengeance.
2. Even the pure Immortals cannot escape it.
3. Last song of the play; usually contains a moral lesson
4. Purification of a character's emotions; an emotional release
5. According to Creon, all prophets love this.
6. Engaged to Antigone; son of Creon
7. Movement of the chorus from right to left across the stage
8. Teiresias heard these & they frightened him.
9. Collection of plays submitted in the Dionysia competition
10. God's crowning gift to man, according to Haimon
11. Creon decreed it illegal to ___ Polyneices.
12. Those who anger him will suffer his wrath.
13. One of man's accomplishments: he conquered the ___
14. Introduces the main characters at the beginning of the play
15. Play that comically portrayed mythological stories or poked fun at politics
16. Group that sings and comments on the actions of the characters

| A=2 | B=3 | C=15 | D=14 |
| --- | --- | --- | --- |
| E=13 | F=16 | G=4 | H=1 |
| I=8 | J=5 | K=9 | L=12 |
| M=11 | N=10 | O=6 | P=7 |

Antigone Word Search 1

```
E  B  Y  E  G  A  U  G  N  A  L  C  H  O  R  U  S  E  N  V
T  M  K  R  J  E  H  A  R  M  A  R  T  I  A  E  H  V  Q  Z
E  T  K  X  D  S  G  A  N  T  I  S  T  R  O  P  H  E  S  S
O  P  T  X  P  C  M  O  Z  X  P  S  T  T  O  I  X  O  B  E
C  B  L  R  F  H  F  W  D  F  R  A  E  R  G  S  G  J  V  E
L  J  E  U  R  Y  D  I  C  E  S  A  T  Y  R  O  Z  O  N  K
E  E  T  H  X  L  S  Z  T  N  S  S  R  H  L  D  L  E  J  T
S  T  P  U  Z  U  B  S  Y  O  Q  W  A  T  O  E  M  D  H  Y
T  H  E  B  E  S  I  E  U  G  O  L  O  R  P  S  G  O  D  S
S  O  A  R  S  R  B  S  I  J  B  L  A  I  U  C  R  I  P
U  S  X  I  F  Q  D  U  E  T  R  P  O  G  D  E  R  E  O  D
D  S  M  S  M  L  S  R  A  N  H  A  G  E  E  Z  E  A  N  M
O  I  M  B  X  O  D  Y  S  A  G  E  Y  D  A  Z  O  S  Y  P
X  W  O  H  H  J  N  M  Y  M  V  A  S  Y  T  Q  N  O  S  X
E  X  F  N  L  B  A  T  T  L  E  N  L  P  H  C  X  N  O  X
Z  S  T  U  Y  D  S  O  D  A  R  A  P  R  I  P  P  K  S  Y
V  W  O  Z  Q  S  H  T  Z  L  H  M  P  Z  G  S  S  M  Y  T
W  S  L  V  Q  H  I  Z  L  R  J  O  E  D  I  P  U  S  R  Q
T  E  I  R  E  S  I  A  S  C  A  T  H  A  R  S  I  S  W  D
```

According to Creon, all prophets love this. (4)
Arrogance demonstrated by a character as a result of his/her pride or passion (6)
Attempt to appeal to one's sense of moral duty as persuasion (5)
Attempt to use emotion as a means of persuasion (6)
Attempt to use reason as a means of persuasion (5)
Blind prophet (9)
Collection of plays submitted in the Dionysia competition (10)
Considered to be the Father of Greek Theater (7)
Creon decreed it illegal to ___ Polyneices. (4)
Engaged to Antigone; son of Creon (6)
Even the pure Immortals cannot escape it. (4)
Festival honoring the Greek God of wine (8)
God of wine in whose honor Greek tragedies were performed (8)
God's crowning gift to man, according to Haimon (6)
Greek playwright who was defeated in the tetralogy competition by Sophocles (9)
Group that sings and comments on the actions of the characters (6)
Ill-fated daughter of Oedipus; defied the king's decree (8)
Introduces the main characters at the beginning of the play (8)
It has seven gates in a yawning ring. (6)
Killed his father & married his mother; father of Antigone (7)
Last song of the play; usually contains a moral lesson (6)
Movement of the chorus from left to right across the stage (11)
Movement of the chorus from right to left across the stage (7)
Oedipus's 2 sons were killed in ___. (6)
Oedipus's son buried with full honors (8)
One of man's accomplishments: he conquered the ___ (4)
One of man's accomplishments: he created ___ (8)
Opening song as the chorus makes its entrance (7)
Penalty for burying Polyneices (5)
Play that comically portrayed mythological stories or poked fun at politics (5)
Prayer of thanksgiving to Dionysos at the end of the play (5)
Purification of a character's emotions; an emotional release (9)
Queen of Thebes (8)
Refused to help her sister bury Polyneices (6)
Relationship between Antigone and Ismene (7)
Scene in a play (7)
Serious play in which the main character suffers from a flaw (7)
Songs that comment on the action of the play or its characters (4)
Teiresias heard these & they frightened him. (5)
The fortunate man is one who has never tasted ___'s vengeance. (3)
Those who anger him will suffer his wrath. (4)
Took over as King of Thebes after the war (5)
Tragic flaw in a character's personality (9)
When his body was buried, Polyneices's ___ could move to the Underworld. (4)
___ is the most wonderful of all the world's wonders. (3)

Antigone Word Search 1 Answer Key

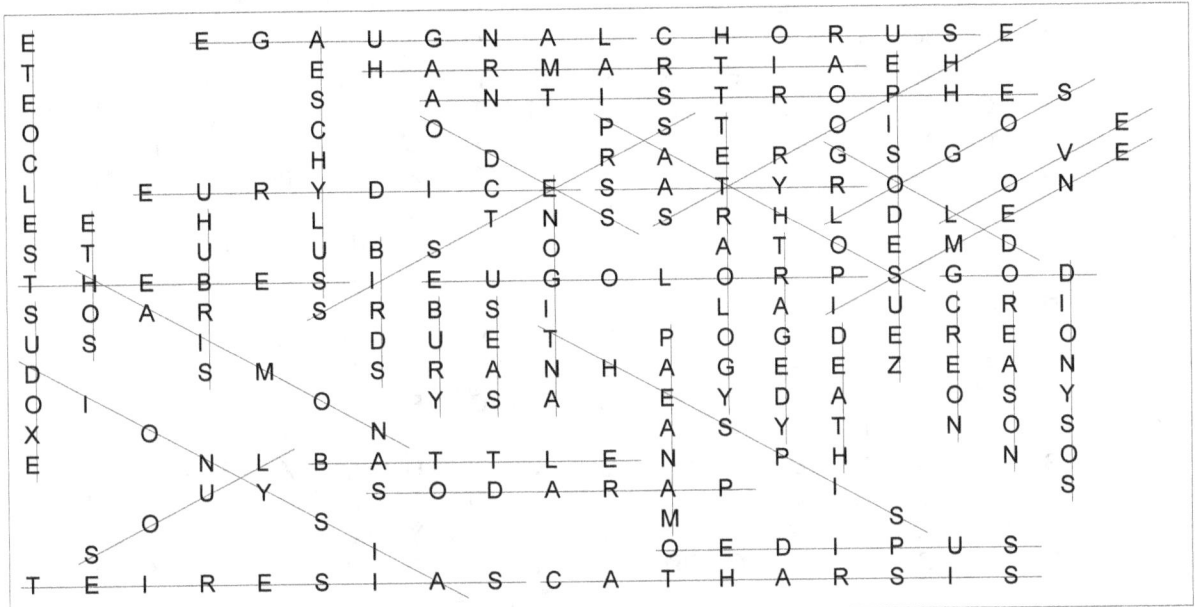

According to Creon, all prophets love this. (4)
Arrogance demonstrated by a character as a result of his/her pride or passion (6)
Attempt to appeal to one's sense of moral duty as persuasion (5)
Attempt to use emotion as a means of persuasion (6)
Attempt to use reason as a means of persuasion (5)
Blind prophet (9)
Collection of plays submitted in the Dionysia competition (10)
Considered to be the Father of Greek Theater (7)
Creon decreed it illegal to ___ Polyneices. (4)
Engaged to Antigone; son of Creon (6)
Even the pure Immortals cannot escape it. (4)
Festival honoring the Greek God of wine (8)
God of wine in whose honor Greek tragedies were performed (8)
God's crowning gift to man, according to Haimon (6)
Greek playwright who was defeated in the tetralogy competition by Sophocles (9)
Group that sings and comments on the actions of the characters (6)
Ill-fated daughter of Oedipus; defied the king's decree (8)
Introduces the main characters at the beginning of the play (8)
It has seven gates in a yawning ring. (6)
Killed his father & married his mother; father of Antigone (7)
Last song of the play; usually contains a moral lesson (6)
Movement of the chorus from left to right across the stage (11)
Movement of the chorus from right to left across the stage (7)
Oedipus's 2 sons were killed in ___. (6)
Oedipus's son buried with full honors (8)
One of man's accomplishments: he conquered the ___ (4)
One of man's accomplishments: he created ___ (8)
Opening song as the chorus makes its entrance (7)
Penalty for burying Polyneices (5)
Play that comically portrayed mythological stories or poked fun at politics (5)
Prayer of thanksgiving to Dionysos at the end of the play (5)
Purification of a character's emotions; an emotional release (9)
Queen of Thebes (8)
Refused to help her sister bury Polyneices (6)
Relationship between Antigone and Ismene (7)
Scene in a play (7)
Serious play in which the main character suffers from a flaw (7)
Songs that comment on the action of the play or its characters (4)
Teiresias heard these & they frightened him. (5)
The fortunate man is one who has never tasted ___'s vengeance. (3)
Those who anger him will suffer his wrath. (4)
Took over as King of Thebes after the war (5)
Tragic flaw in a character's personality (9)
When his body was buried, Polyneices's ___ could move to the Underworld. (4)
___ is the most wonderful of all the world's wonders. (3)

Antigone Word Search 2

```
P A E A N T I S T R O P H E B E S M
P A R X H R H E R V D H H D N U A E
P R T C K T M U A E M T H E R T Z
O B O H L R E G T A T M O S E Y Y
L A B L O V V Y E E N S H F O X R Q
Y T C N O S C D I I C O C G S X Z
N T A L S G Q I R C D L N A I J Q
E L T P I Q U C Y E P E W X R S O S
I E H A P C W E F S S T T V O T E Z
C V A R S M L T Y I E W J H H E D Y
E K R A E J P O H A T J T E C R I M
S P S D H Q T A G S H C B D M S P T
V H I O T U I X L O O E S L Y S U T
T H S S S M B I R D S U D O X E S J
R L E A O U V R J Z Z O T G U U K H
S D E N R D B M I B G J Y L E L W H
O S C Y C R E O N S H Z S Z B Z H Y
```

According to Creon, all prophets love this. (4)
Arrogance demonstrated by a character as a result of his/her pride or passion (6)
Attempt to appeal to one's sense of moral duty as persuasion (5)
Attempt to use emotion as a means of persuasion (6)
Attempt to use reason as a means of persuasion (5)
Blind prophet (9)
Considered a traitor to Thebes; his body was left to rot (10)
Considered to be the Father of Greek Theater (7)
Creon decreed it illegal to ___ Polyneices. (4)
Engaged to Antigone; son of Creon (6)
Even the pure Immortals cannot escape it. (4)
God's crowning gift to man, according to Haimon (6)
Group that sings and comments on the actions of the characters (6)
Introduces the main characters at the beginning of the play (8)
It has seven gates in a yawning ring. (6)
Killed his father & married his mother; father of Antigone (7)
Last song of the play; usually contains a moral lesson (6)
Leader of the chorus (8)
Movement of the chorus from left to right across the stage (11)
Movement of the chorus from right to left across the stage (7)
Oedipus's 2 sons were killed in ___. (6)
Oedipus's son buried with full honors (8)
One of man's accomplishments: he conquered the ___ (4)
Opening song as the chorus makes its entrance (7)
Penalty for burying Polyneices (5)
Play that comically portrayed mythological stories or poked fun at politics (5)
Prayer of thanksgiving to Dionysos at the end of the play (5)
Purification of a character's emotions; an emotional release (9)
Queen of Thebes (8)
Refused to help her sister bury Polyneices (6)
Relationship between Antigone and Ismene (7)
Scene in a play (7)
Serious play in which the main character suffers from a flaw (7)
Songs that comment on the action of the play or its characters (4)
Teiresias heard these & they frightened him. (5)
The fortunate man is one who has never tasted ___'s vengeance. (3)
Those who anger him will suffer his wrath. (4)
Took over as King of Thebes after the war (5)
When his body was buried, Polyneices's ___ could move to the Underworld. (4)
___ is the most wonderful of all the world's wonders. (3)

Antigone Word Search 2 Answer Key

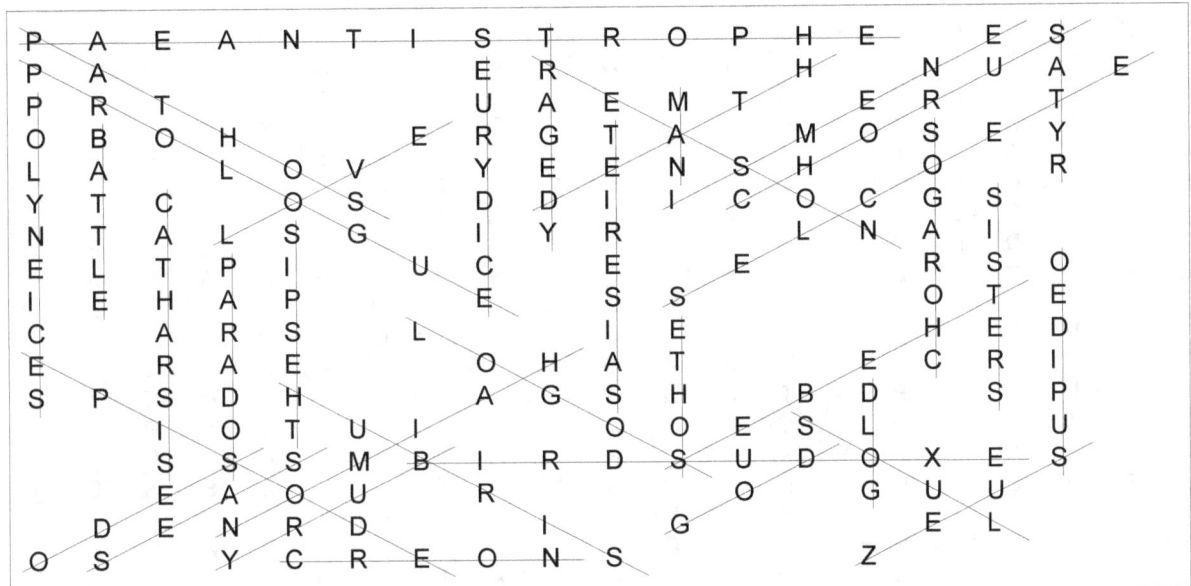

According to Creon, all prophets love this. (4)
Arrogance demonstrated by a character as a result of his/her pride or passion (6)
Attempt to appeal to one's sense of moral duty as persuasion (5)
Attempt to use emotion as a means of persuasion (6)
Attempt to use reason as a means of persuasion (5)
Blind prophet (9)
Considered a traitor to Thebes; his body was left to rot (10)
Considered to be the Father of Greek Theater (7)
Creon decreed it illegal to ___ Polyneices. (4)
Engaged to Antigone; son of Creon (6)
Even the pure Immortals cannot escape it. (4)
God's crowning gift to man, according to Haimon (6)
Group that sings and comments on the actions of the characters (6)
Introduces the main characters at the beginning of the play (8)
It has seven gates in a yawning ring. (6)
Killed his father & married his mother; father of Antigone (7)
Last song of the play; usually contains a moral lesson (6)
Leader of the chorus (8)
Movement of the chorus from left to right across the stage (11)
Movement of the chorus from right to left across the stage (7)
Oedipus's 2 sons were killed in ___. (6)
Oedipus's son buried with full honors (8)
One of man's accomplishments: he conquered the ___ (4)
Opening song as the chorus makes its entrance (7)
Penalty for burying Polyneices (5)
Play that comically portrayed mythological stories or poked fun at politics (5)
Prayer of thanksgiving to Dionysos at the end of the play (5)
Purification of a character's emotions; an emotional release (9)
Queen of Thebes (8)
Refused to help her sister bury Polyneices (6)
Relationship between Antigone and Ismene (7)
Scene in a play (7)
Serious play in which the main character suffers from a flaw (7)
Songs that comment on the action of the play or its characters (4)
Teiresias heard these & they frightened him. (5)
The fortunate man is one who has never tasted ___'s vengeance. (3)
Those who anger him will suffer his wrath. (4)
Took over as King of Thebes after the war (5)
When his body was buried, Polyneices's ___ could move to the Underworld. (4)
___ is the most wonderful of all the world's wonders. (3)

## Antigone Word Search 3

```
P Q N E H C F J P G Z G P N S A B D P P
O S I S T E R H Z O P H E U N U E A T
L S K T E H O T O V P A N P T R A L
Y V X T E Z P L V D B E I I A E H
N P E A I R X P D U R S M D S S H N L
E D L G E G E S B Q L R B S E T G O Z H
I X T E S D D S M D A Q I O R C W D V
C H T D I D R J F O R S N J P O N C P R
E A A Y A D I O N Y S O S S R P M A N E
S N B I S X B O T V H N U O O H E T N J
Y T V F M S K A N H G R L G L E U H H V
T I C C V O S T E Y O L O A O A R A E B
X G L R J P N T F H S V V R G E Y R S W
T O T Z E H E T G S K I E O U S D P L
Z N H M D O Y X C C R Y A H E C I I I F
J E E Z C C N H E N B Y I C S H C S S D
C B B L J L X S T K L D T F F Y E P I W
X L E N R E X N R D N P R Y J L C Z R Q
J S S D Q S O D A R A P A R C U R X B N
Z S N S G U K P O P H S M T S S F P U N
K W P T D D P M L H V B R W H S F Q H Z
P D K L H O Y M O V D C A X O O C M G Z
K Y L J L X W T G D M W H G Y D S C J D
F R Q K H E B S Y W P Z O T X X C J G N
L A N G U A G E J P G L G Q V B J W Q D
```

| AESCHYLUS | DEATH | HAIMON | PAEAN | SOUL |
| ANTIGONE | DIONYSIA | HARMARTIA | PARADOS | STROPHE |
| ANTISTROPHE | DIONYSOS | HUBRIS | PATHOS | TEIRESIAS |
| BATTLE | EPISODE | ISMENE | POLYNEICES | TETRAOLOGY |
| BIRDS | ETEOCLES | LANGUAGE | PROLOGUE | THEBES |
| BURY | ETHOS | LOGOS | REASON | THESPIS |
| CATHARSIS | EURYDICE | LOVE | SATYR | TRAGEDY |
| CHORAGOS | EXODUS | MAN | SEAS | ZEUS |
| CHORUS | GOD | ODES | SISTERS | |
| CREON | GOLD | OEDIPUS | SOPHOCLES | |

Antigone Word Search 3 Answer Key

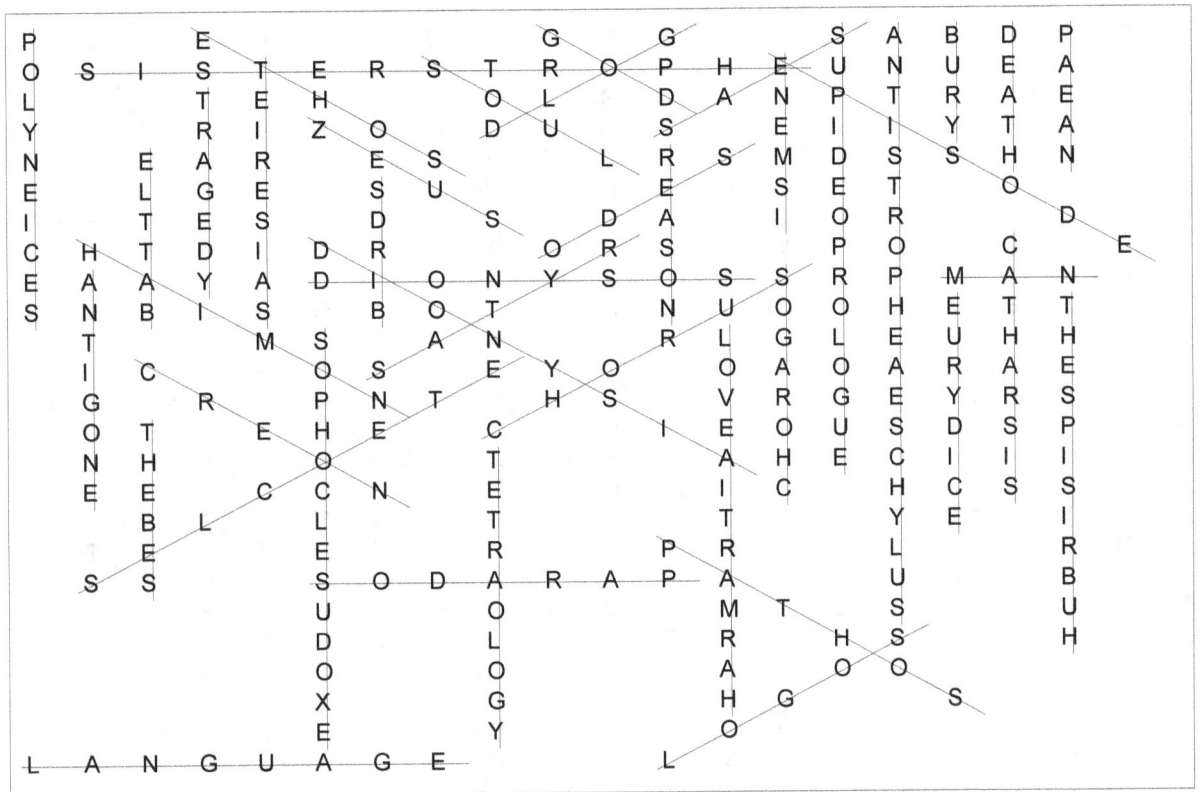

| AESCHYLUS | DEATH | HAIMON | PAEAN | SOUL |
| ANTIGONE | DIONYSIA | HARMARTIA | PARADOS | STROPHE |
| ANTISTROPHE | DIONYSOS | HUBRIS | PATHOS | TEIRESIAS |
| BATTLE | EPISODE | ISMENE | POLYNEICES | TETRAOLOGY |
| BIRDS | ETEOCLES | LANGUAGE | PROLOGUE | THEBES |
| BURY | ETHOS | LOGOS | REASON | THESPIS |
| CATHARSIS | EURYDICE | LOVE | SATYR | TRAGEDY |
| CHORAGOS | EXODUS | MAN | SEAS | ZEUS |
| CHORUS | GOD | ODES | SISTERS | |
| CREON | GOLD | OEDIPUS | SOPHOCLES | |

## Antigone Word Search 4

```
P D I O N Y S I A P H L A N G U A G E M
M A Y F V L G A S R A D Y N Z W Q T U F
N D R B C L G E O O H I P Z B K F H R W
G V Z A G C Z S P L M O T R A G E D Y Q
A P C N D Y S C H O A N H P B R Z H D Y
K N Z G D O Q H O G R Y U L M Q N V I Q
L N T M Y Y S Y C U T S B M L X S J C W
P C T I A T B L E I O R G L C Y W E F
H L T W G N Z U E K A S I H X N Z T V G
T P L B V O T S S C F Y S G K G S Z K X
K E F J S L N I T E M R A O L O G Y D J
S B I G C O M E S M M E D K G N B S S V
Q S X R Q G H F F T F T C A O Q B O J R
B H R J E O Z B E W R H X F L Y L H Y B
C H O R U S U P I D E O X X D E A T H X
S E B M U D I S R R H S P O R F A X V
I Y T D J S Y A J C D D G H B S Z P M Q
P M O E O Y B N S S M S F N E I H R A T
S X X D O S L E O S R E T S I S M E N E
E L E D P C L U N L V B D K A R H H O Q
H R B N T L O Z O L E X E V A H Q P E V
T S P A T Z S E L J F H S Y I H D O R M
W M E A Y A E B S F J T R M G T C R C M
C A B T E W B U D G F U O S H A S T N Z
P F Q R P Q G K S S B N R X L C J S B R
```

| AESCHYLUS | DEATH | HAIMON | PAEAN | STROPHE |
| ANTIGONE | DIONYSIA | HARMARTIA | PARADOS | TEIRESIAS |
| ANTISTROPHE | DIONYSOS | HUBRIS | PATHOS | TETRAOLOGY |
| BATTLE | EPISODE | ISMENE | PROLOGUE | THEBES |
| BIRDS | ETEOCLES | LANGUAGE | REASON | THESPIS |
| BURY | ETHOS | LOGOS | SATYR | TRAGEDY |
| CATHARSIS | EURYDICE | LOVE | SEAS | ZEUS |
| CHORAGOS | EXODUS | MAN | SISTERS | |
| CHORUS | GOD | ODES | SOPHOCLES | |
| CREON | GOLD | OEDIPUS | SOUL | |

Antigone Word Search 4 Answer Key

| AESCHYLUS | DEATH | HAIMON | PAEAN | STROPHE |
| ANTIGONE | DIONYSIA | HARMARTIA | PARADOS | TEIRESIAS |
| ANTISTROPHE | DIONYSOS | HUBRIS | PATHOS | TETRAOLOGY |
| BATTLE | EPISODE | ISMENE | PROLOGUE | THEBES |
| BIRDS | ETEOCLES | LANGUAGE | REASON | THESPIS |
| BURY | ETHOS | LOGOS | SATYR | TRAGEDY |
| CATHARSIS | EURYDICE | LOVE | SEAS | ZEUS |
| CHORAGOS | EXODUS | MAN | SISTERS | |
| CHORUS | GOD | ODES | SOPHOCLES | |
| CREON | GOLD | OEDIPUS | SOUL | |

# Antigone Crossword 1

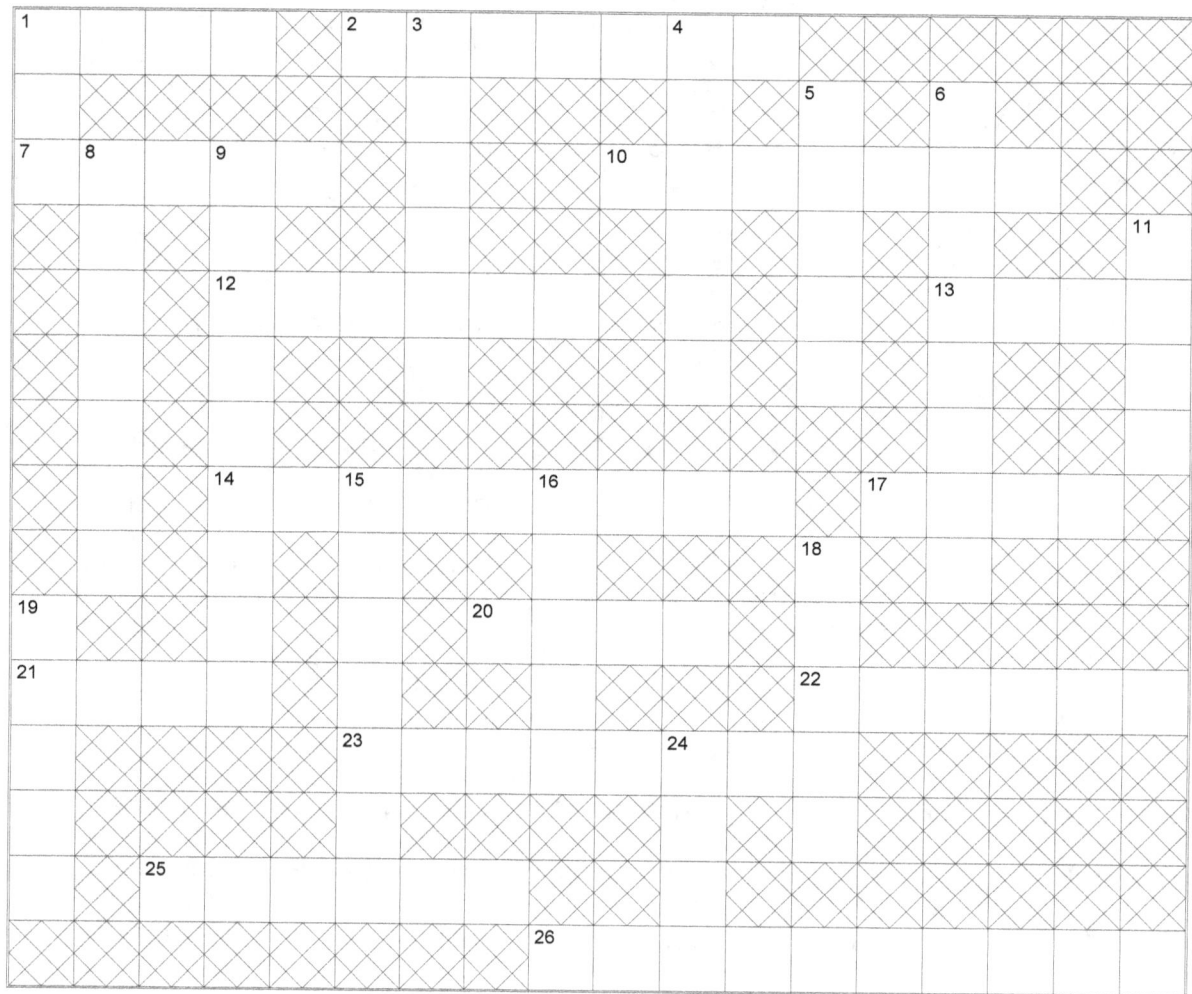

**Across**
1. According to Creon, all prophets love this.
2. Movement of the chorus from right to left across the stage
7. Penalty for burying Polyneices
10. Relationship between Antigone and Ismene
12. Refused to help her sister bury Polyneices
13. Even the pure Immortals cannot escape it.
14. Author of the play Antigone
17. Creon decreed it illegal to ___ Polyneices.
20. Those who anger him will suffer his wrath.
21. Songs that comment on the action of the play or its characters
22. Last song of the play; usually contains a moral lesson
23. Festival honoring the Greek God of wine
25. God's crowning gift to man, according to Haimon
26. Considered a traitor to Thebes; his body was left to rot

**Down**
1. The fortunate man is one who has never tasted ___'s vengeance.
3. It has seven gates in a yawning ring.
4. Engaged to Antigone; son of Creon
5. Attempt to appeal to one's sense of moral duty as persuasion
6. Introduces the main characters at the beginning of the play
8. Scene in a play
9. Blind prophet
11. One of man's accomplishments: he conquered the ___
15. Opening song as the chorus makes its entrance
16. Took over as King of Thebes after the war
18. Prayer of thanksgiving to Dionysos at the end of the play
19. Attempt to use reason as a means of persuasion
24. When his body was buried, Polyneices's ___ could move to the Underworld.

# Antigone Crossword 1 Answer Key

|   | 1 G | O | L | D |   | 2 S | 3 T | R | O | P | 4 H | E |   |   |   |   |
|---|---|---|---|---|---|---|---|---|---|---|---|---|---|---|---|---|
|   | O |   |   |   |   |   | H |   |   |   | A |   | 5 E |   | 6 P |   |
| 7 D | 8 E | A | 9 T | H |   |   | E |   |   | 10 S | I | S | T | E | R | S |
|   | P |   | E |   |   |   | B |   |   | M |   | H |   | O |   | 11 S |
|   | I |   | 12 I | S | M | E | N | E |   | O |   | O |   | 13 L | O | V | E |
|   | S |   | R |   |   |   | S |   |   | N |   | S |   | O |   | A |
|   | O |   | E |   |   |   |   |   |   |   |   |   |   | G |   | S |
|   |   |   | 14 D | 15 S | O | P | H | 16 O | C | L | E | S |   | 17 B | U | R | Y |
|   |   |   | E |   | I |   |   | A |   | R |   |   | 18 P |   | E |   |
| 19 L |   |   |   |   | A |   |   | 20 Z | E | U | S |   | A |   |   |   |
| 21 O | D | E | S |   | A |   |   | O |   |   |   | 22 E | X | O | D | U | S |
| G |   |   |   |   | 23 D | I | O | N | Y | 24 S | I | A |   |   |   |   |
| O |   |   |   |   | O |   |   |   |   | O |   | N |   |   |   |   |
| S |   | 25 R | E | A | S | O | N |   |   | U |   |   |   |   |   |   |
|   |   |   |   |   |   |   |   | 26 P | O | L | Y | N | E | I | C | E | S |

**Across**
1. According to Creon, all prophets love this.
2. Movement of the chorus from right to left across the stage
7. Penalty for burying Polyneices
10. Relationship between Antigone and Ismene
12. Refused to help her sister bury Polyneices
13. Even the pure Immortals cannot escape it.
14. Author of the play Antigone
17. Creon decreed it illegal to ___ Polyneices.
20. Those who anger him will suffer his wrath.
21. Songs that comment on the action of the play or its characters
22. Last song of the play; usually contains a moral lesson
23. Festival honoring the Greek God of wine
25. God's crowning gift to man, according to Haimon
26. Considered a traitor to Thebes; his body was left to rot

**Down**
1. The fortunate man is one who has never tasted ___'s vengeance.
3. It has seven gates in a yawning ring.
4. Engaged to Antigone; son of Creon
5. Attempt to appeal to one's sense of moral duty as persuasion
6. Introduces the main characters at the beginning of the play
8. Scene in a play
9. Blind prophet
11. One of man's accomplishments: he conquered the ___
15. Opening song as the chorus makes its entrance
16. Took over as King of Thebes after the war
18. Prayer of thanksgiving to Dionysos at the end of the play
19. Attempt to use reason as a means of persuasion
24. When his body was buried, Polyneices's ___ could move to the Underworld.

# Antigone Crossword 2

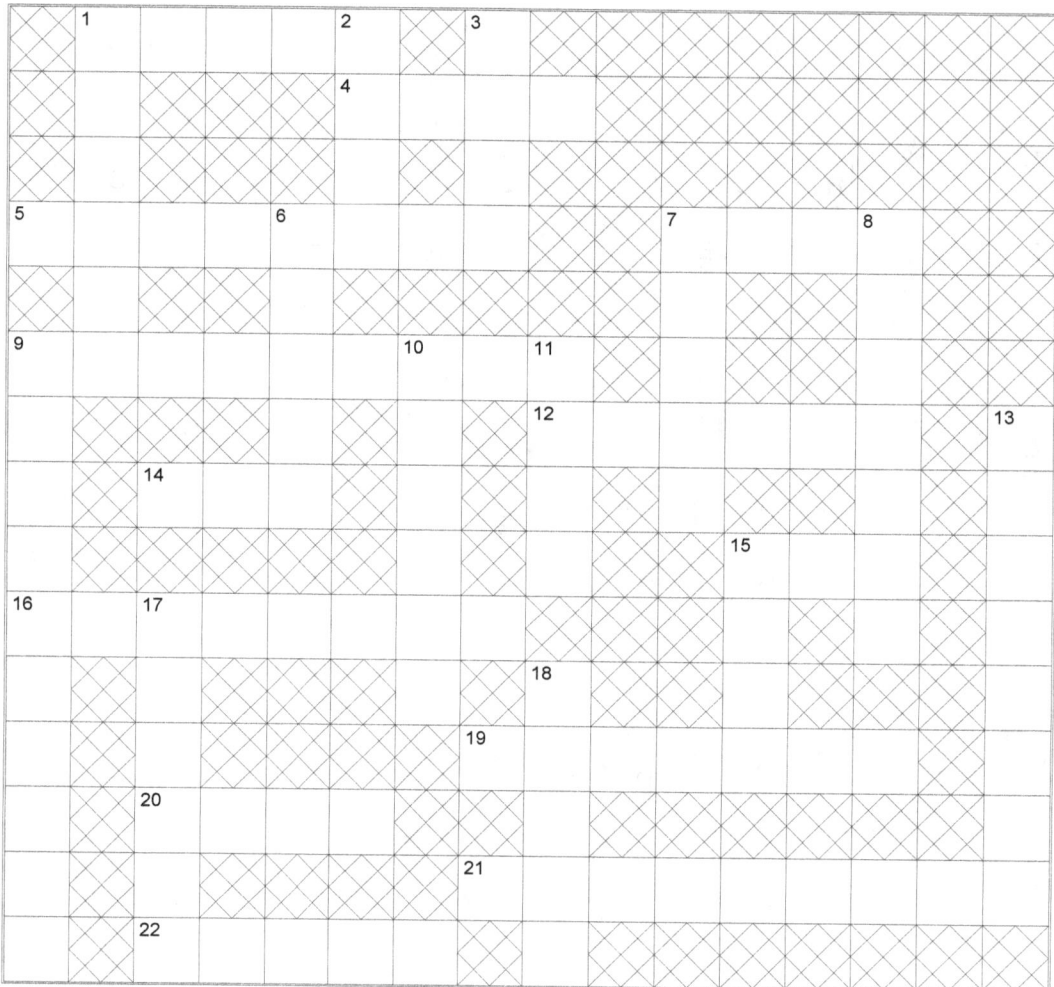

**Across**
1. Teiresias heard these & they frightened him.
4. Songs that comment on the action of the play or its characters
5. Oedipus's son buried with full honors
7. Even the pure Immortals cannot escape it.
9. Blind prophet
12. Last song of the play; usually contains a moral lesson
14. ___ is the most wonderful of all the world's wonders.
15. The fortunate man is one who has never tasted ___'s vengeance.
16. Ill-fated daughter of Oedipus; defied the king's decree
19. Opening song as the chorus makes its entrance
20. Creon decreed it illegal to ___ Polyneices.
21. Tragic flaw in a character's personality
22. Play that comically portrayed mythological stories or poked fun at politics

**Down**
1. Oedipus's 2 sons were killed in ___.
2. When his body was buried, Polyneices's ___ could move to the Underworld.
3. Those who anger him will suffer his wrath.
6. Took over as King of Thebes after the war
7. Attempt to use reason as a means of persuasion
8. Scene in a play
9. Collection of plays submitted in the Dionysia competition
10. Refused to help her sister bury Polyneices
11. One of man's accomplishments: he conquered the ___
13. Festival honoring the Greek God of wine
15. According to Creon, all prophets love this.
17. It has seven gates in a yawning ring.
18. Prayer of thanksgiving to Dionysos at the end of the play

Antigone Crossword 2 Answer Key

|   | 1 B | I | R | 2 D S | 3 Z |   |   |   |   |
|---|---|---|---|---|---|---|---|---|---|
|   | A |   |   | 4 O | D | E | S |   |   |
|   | T |   |   | U |   | U |   |   |   |
| 5 E | T | E | O | 6 C | L | E | S |   | 7 L | O | V | 8 E |
|   | L |   |   | R |   |   |   | O |   | P |
| 9 T | E | I | R | E | S | 10 I | A | 11 S |   | G |   |   | I |
| E |   |   |   | O |   | S |   | 12 E | X | O | D | U | S | 13 D |
| T |   | 14 M | A | N |   | M |   | A |   | S |   |   | O |   | I |
| R |   |   |   |   |   | E |   | S |   |   | 15 G | O | D |   | O |
| 16 A | N | 17 T | I | G | O | N | E |   |   |   | O |   | E |   | N |
| O |   | H |   |   |   | E |   | 18 P |   |   | L |   |   |   | Y |
| L |   | E |   |   |   | 19 P | A | R | A | D | O | S |   |   | S |
| O |   | 20 B | U | R | Y |   |   | E |   |   |   |   |   |   | I |
| G |   | E |   |   |   |   |   | 21 H | A | R | M | A | R | T | I | A |
| Y |   | 22 S | A | T | Y | R |   | N |   |   |   |   |   |   |

Across
1. Teiresias heard these & they frightened him.
4. Songs that comment on the action of the play or its characters
5. Oedipus's son buried with full honors
7. Even the pure Immortals cannot escape it.
9. Blind prophet
12. Last song of the play; usually contains a moral lesson
14. ___ is the most wonderful of all the world's wonders.
15. The fortunate man is one who has never tasted ___'s vengeance.
16. Ill-fated daughter of Oedipus; defied the king's decree
19. Opening song as the chorus makes its entrance
20. Creon decreed it illegal to ___ Polyneices.
21. Tragic flaw in a character's personality
22. Play that comically portrayed mythological stories or poked fun at politics

Down
1. Oedipus's 2 sons were killed in ___.
2. When his body was buried, Polyneices's ___ could move to the Underworld.
3. Those who anger him will suffer his wrath.
6. Took over as King of Thebes after the war
7. Attempt to use reason as a means of persuasion
8. Scene in a play
9. Collection of plays submitted in the Dionysia competition
10. Refused to help her sister bury Polyneices
11. One of man's accomplishments: he conquered the ___
13. Festival honoring the Greek God of wine
15. According to Creon, all prophets love this.
17. It has seven gates in a yawning ring.
18. Prayer of thanksgiving to Dionysos at the end of the play

# Antigone Crossword 3

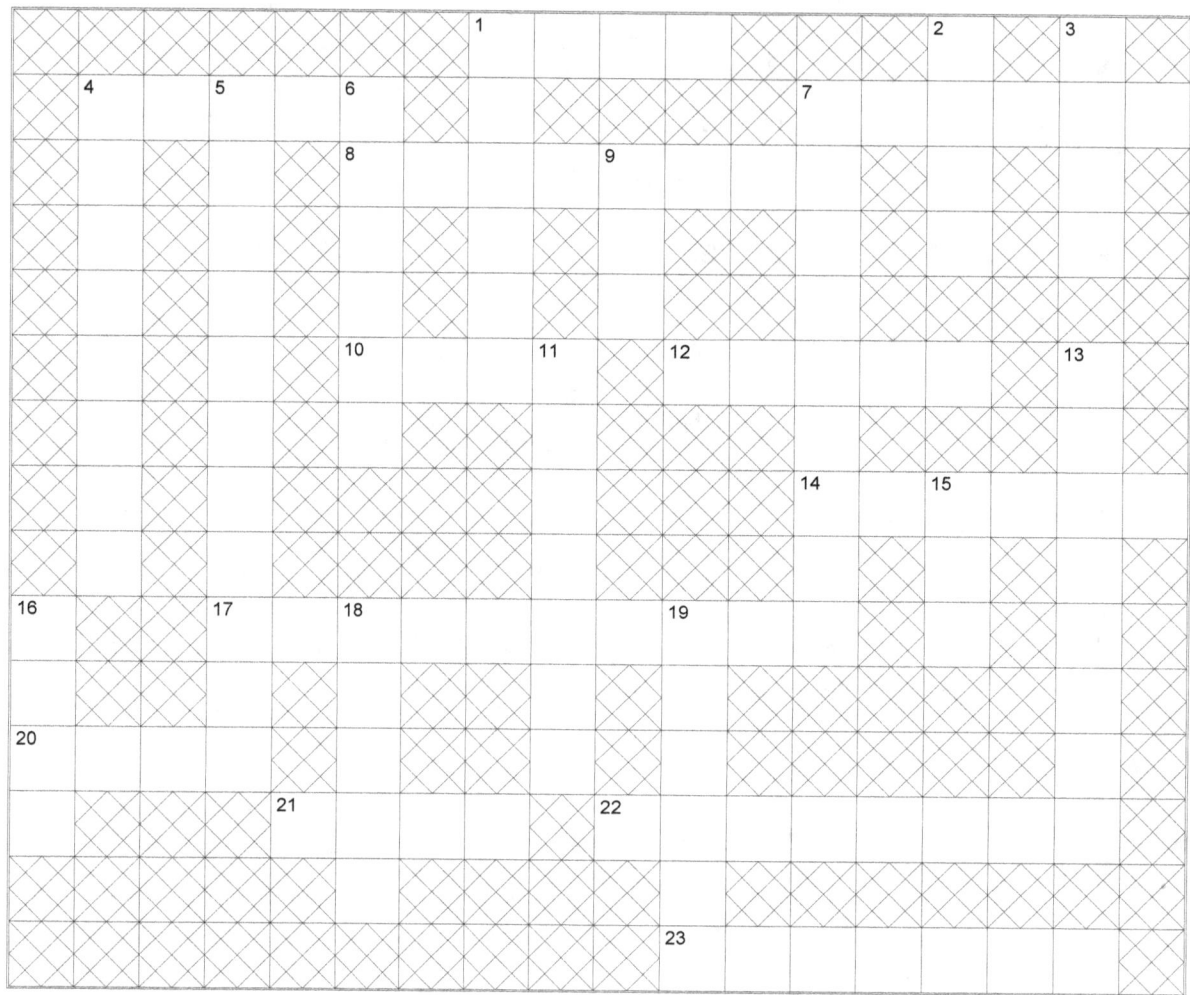

## Across

1. Creon decreed it illegal to ___ Polyneices.
4. Penalty for burying Polyneices
7. It has seven gates in a yawning ring.
8. Ill-fated daughter of Oedipus; defied the king's decree
10. Songs that comment on the action of the play or its characters
12. Prayer of thanksgiving to Dionysos at the end of the play
14. Refused to help her sister bury Polyneices
17. Considered a traitor to Thebes; his body was left to rot
20. Even the pure Immortals cannot escape it.
21. When his body was buried, Polyneices's ___ could move to the Underworld.
22. Introduces the main characters at the beginning of the play
23. Movement of the chorus from right to left across the stage

## Down

1. Oedipus's 2 sons were killed in ___.
2. One of man's accomplishments: he conquered the ___
3. Those who anger him will suffer his wrath.
4. Festival honoring the Greek God of wine
5. Movement of the chorus from left to right across the stage
6. Engaged to Antigone; son of Creon
7. Blind prophet
9. The fortunate man is one who has never tasted ___'s vengeance.
11. Relationship between Antigone and Ismene
13. One of man's accomplishments: he created ___
15. ___ is the most wonderful of all the world's wonders.
16. According to Creon, all prophets love this.
18. Attempt to use reason as a means of persuasion
19. Group that sings and comments on the actions of the characters

Antigone Crossword 3 Answer Key

|   |   |   |   |   |   | 1 B | U | R | Y |   |   | 2 S |   | 3 Z |   |
|---|---|---|---|---|---|---|---|---|---|---|---|---|---|---|---|
|   | 4 D | E | 5 A | T | 6 H |   | A |   |   |   | 7 T | H | E | B | E | S |
|   | I |   | N |   | 8 A | N | T | 9 I | G | O | N | E |   | A |   | U |
|   | O |   | T |   | I |   |   | T |   | O |   | I |   | S |   | S |
|   | N |   | I |   | M |   |   | L |   | D |   | R |   |   |   |   |
|   | Y |   | S |   | 10 O | D | 11 E | S |   | 12 P | A | E | A | N |   | 13 L |
|   | S |   | T |   | N |   | I |   |   |   | S |   |   |   |   | A |
|   |   |   |   |   |   |   |   |   |   |   | 14 I |   | 15 S | M | E | N | E |
|   | I |   | R |   |   |   | S |   |   |   |   |   | M |   |   | A |
|   | A |   | O |   |   |   | T |   |   |   | A |   | A |   |   | G |
| 16 G |   | 17 P | O | 18 L | Y | N | E | I | 19 C | E | S |   | N |   |   | U |
| O |   | H |   | O |   |   | R |   | H |   |   |   |   |   |   | A |
| 20 L | O | V | E |   |   |   | S |   | O |   |   |   |   |   |   | G |
| D |   |   |   | 21 S | O | U | L |   | 22 P | R | O | L | O | G | U | E |
|   |   |   |   | S |   |   |   |   | U |   |   |   |   |   |   |   |
|   |   |   |   |   |   |   |   |   | 23 S | T | R | O | P | H | E |   |

Across
1. Creon decreed it illegal to ___ Polyneices.
4. Penalty for burying Polyneices
7. It has seven gates in a yawning ring.
8. Ill-fated daughter of Oedipus; defied the king's decree
10. Songs that comment on the action of the play or its characters
12. Prayer of thanksgiving to Dionysos at the end of the play
14. Refused to help her sister bury Polyneices
17. Considered a traitor to Thebes; his body was left to rot
20. Even the pure Immortals cannot escape it.
21. When his body was buried, Polyneices's ___ could move to the Underworld.
22. Introduces the main characters at the beginning of the play
23. Movement of the chorus from right to left across the stage

Down
1. Oedipus's 2 sons were killed in ___.
2. One of man's accomplishments: he conquered the ___
3. Those who anger him will suffer his wrath.
4. Festival honoring the Greek God of wine
5. Movement of the chorus from left to right across the stage
6. Engaged to Antigone; son of Creon
7. Blind prophet
9. The fortunate man is one who has never tasted ___'s vengeance.
11. Relationship between Antigone and Ismene
13. One of man's accomplishments: he created ___
15. ___ is the most wonderful of all the world's wonders.
16. According to Creon, all prophets love this.
18. Attempt to use reason as a means of persuasion
19. Group that sings and comments on the actions of the characters

# Antigone Crossword 4

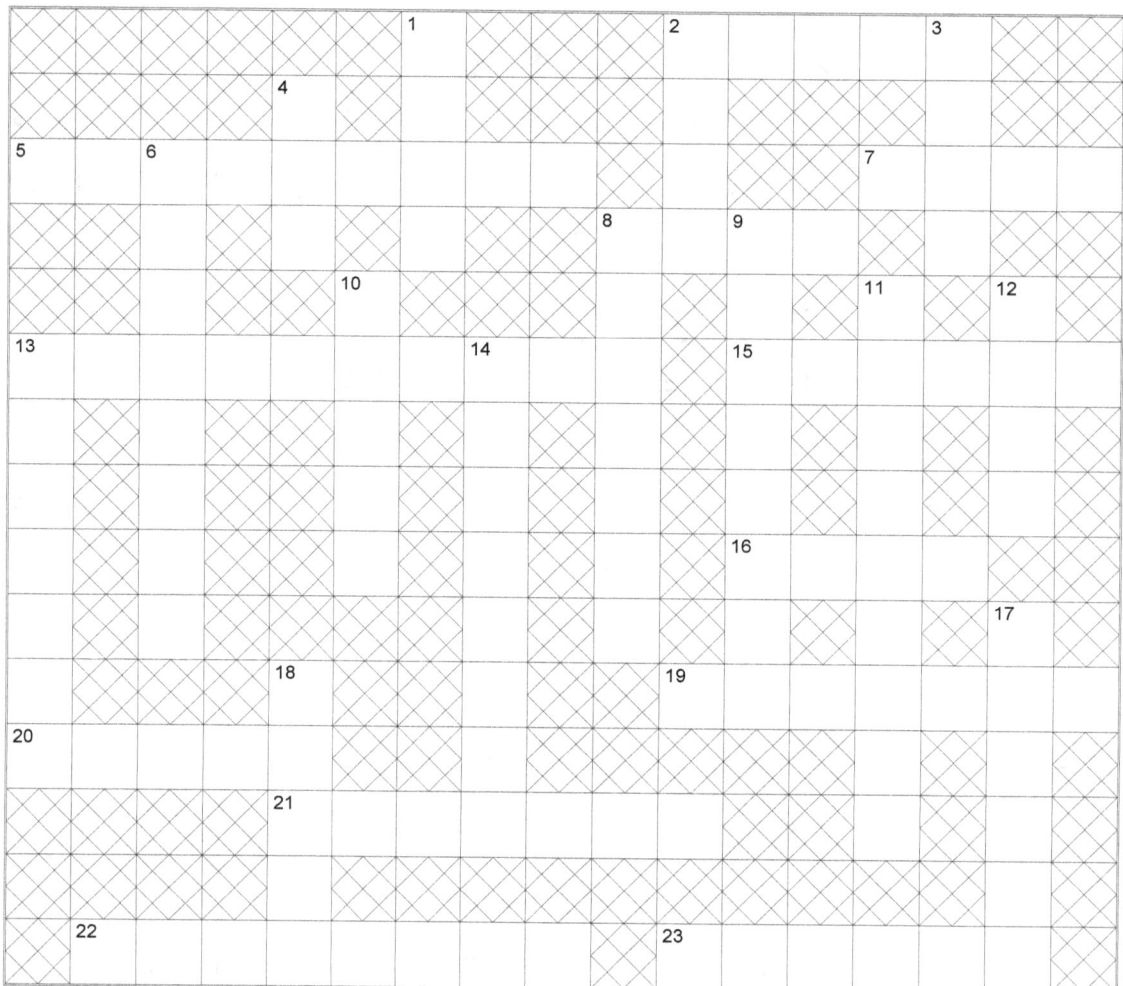

**Across**
2. Attempt to use reason as a means of persuasion
5. Author of the play Antigone
7. Creon decreed it illegal to ___ Polyneices.
8. One of man's accomplishments: he conquered the ___
13. Considered a traitor to Thebes; his body was left to rot
15. It has seven gates in a yawning ring.
16. Songs that comment on the action of the play or its characters
19. Killed his father & married his mother; father of Antigone
20. Play that comically portrayed mythological stories or poked fun at politics
21. Scene in a play
22. Festival honoring the Greek God of wine
23. Group that sings and comments on the actions of the characters

**Down**
1. According to Creon, all prophets love this.
2. Even the pure Immortals cannot escape it.
3. When his body was buried, Polyneices's ___ could move to the Underworld.
4. The fortunate man is one who has never tasted ___'s vengeance.
6. Introduces the main characters at the beginning of the play
8. Relationship between Antigone and Ismene
9. Ill-fated daughter of Oedipus; defied the king's decree
10. Penalty for burying Polyneices
11. Blind prophet
12. Those who anger him will suffer his wrath.
13. Opening song as the chorus makes its entrance
14. Leader of the chorus
17. Arrogance demonstrated by a character as a result of his/her pride or passion
18. Took over as King of Thebes after the war

# Antigone Crossword 4 Answer Key

|   |   |   |   |   |   |   | 1 |   |   | 2 |   |   |   | 3 |   |   |
|---|---|---|---|---|---|---|---|---|---|---|---|---|---|---|---|---|
|   |   |   |   |   |   |   | G |   |   | L | O | G | O | S |   |   |
|   |   |   |   | 4 |   |   | O |   |   | O |   |   |   | O |   |   |
| 5 |   | 6 |   | G | O |   |   |   |   |   |   | 7 |   |   |   |   |
| S | O | P | H | O | C | L | E | S |   | V |   | B | U | R | Y |   |
|   |   | R |   | D |   | D |   | 8 |   | 9 |   | L |   |   |   |   |
|   |   |   |   |   |   |   |   | S | E | A | S |   |   |   |   |   |
|   |   | O |   | 10|   |   |   | I |   | N |   | 11|   | 12|   |   |
|   |   |   |   | D |   |   |   |   |   |   |   | T |   | Z |   |   |
| 13|   |   |   |   |   | 14|   |   |   | 15|   |   |   |   |   |   |
| P | O | L | Y | N | E | I | C | E | S | T | H | E | B | E | S |   |
| A |   | O |   | A |   | H |   | T |   | I |   | I |   | U |   |   |
| R |   | G |   | T |   | O |   | E |   | G |   | R |   | S |   |   |
|   |   |   |   |   |   |   |   |   |   | 16|   |   |   |   |   |   |
| A |   | U |   | H |   | R |   | R |   | O | D | E | S |   |   |   |
|   |   |   |   |   |   |   |   |   |   |   |   |   |   | 17|   |   |
| D |   | E |   |   |   | A |   | S |   | N |   | S |   | H |   |   |
|   |   |   |   | 18|   |   |   |   |   | 19|   |   |   |   |   |   |
| O |   |   |   | C |   | G |   |   |   | O | E | D | I | P | U | S |
| 20|   |   |   |   |   |   |   |   |   |   |   |   |   |   |   |   |
| S | A | T | Y | R |   | O |   |   |   |   |   | A |   | B |   |   |
|   |   |   |   | 21|   |   |   |   |   |   |   |   |   |   |   |   |
|   |   |   |   | E | P | I | S | O | D | E |   | S |   | R |   |   |
|   |   |   |   | O |   |   |   |   |   |   |   |   |   | I |   |   |
|   |   | 22|   |   |   |   |   |   |   | 23|   |   |   |   |   |   |
|   |   | D | I | O | N | Y | S | I | A | C | H | O | R | U | S |   |

**Across**
2. Attempt to use reason as a means of persuasion
5. Author of the play Antigone
7. Creon decreed it illegal to ___ Polyneices.
8. One of man's accomplishments: he conquered the ___
13. Considered a traitor to Thebes; his body was left to rot
15. It has seven gates in a yawning ring.
16. Songs that comment on the action of the play or its characters
19. Killed his father & married his mother; father of Antigone
20. Play that comically portrayed mythological stories or poked fun at politics
21. Scene in a play
22. Festival honoring the Greek God of wine
23. Group that sings and comments on the actions of the characters

**Down**
1. According to Creon, all prophets love this.
2. Even the pure Immortals cannot escape it.
3. When his body was buried, Polyneices's ___ could move to the Underworld.
4. The fortunate man is one who has never tasted ___'s vengeance.
6. Introduces the main characters at the beginning of the play
8. Relationship between Antigone and Ismene
9. Ill-fated daughter of Oedipus; defied the king's decree
10. Penalty for burying Polyneices
11. Blind prophet
12. Those who anger him will suffer his wrath.
13. Opening song as the chorus makes its entrance
14. Leader of the chorus
17. Arrogance demonstrated by a character as a result of his/her pride or passion
18. Took over as King of Thebes after the war

Antigone

| SEAS | DIONYSIA | PARADOS | THESPIS | TEIRESIAS |
|---|---|---|---|---|
| PAEAN | BATTLE | REASON | GOLD | TETRAOLOGY |
| ANTIGONE | PATHOS | FREE SPACE | ETEOCLES | LOVE |
| THEBES | CHORUS | SISTERS | PROLOGUE | SOPHOCLES |
| HARMARTIA | POLYNEICES | EXODUS | LANGUAGE | BIRDS |

Antigone

| DEATH | ANTISTROPHE | STROPHE | OEDIPUS | SATYR |
|---|---|---|---|---|
| EURYDICE | CATHARSIS | LOGOS | TRAGEDY | MAN |
| EPISODE | SOUL | FREE SPACE | ETHOS | GOD |
| HUBRIS | DIONYSOS | AESCHYLUS | BURY | ODES |
| CREON | ZEUS | CHORAGOS | BIRDS | LANGUAGE |

Antigone

| SEAS | ISMENE | AESCHYLUS | STROPHE | CHORAGOS |
| --- | --- | --- | --- | --- |
| CREON | SOUL | ETHOS | DIONYSIA | TETRAOLOGY |
| DIONYSOS | LOGOS | FREE SPACE | THESPIS | PATHOS |
| BURY | MAN | GOD | REASON | CATHARSIS |
| THEBES | GOLD | OEDIPUS | PROLOGUE | EPISODE |

Antigone

| PARADOS | POLYNEICES | ANTIGONE | CHORUS | ZEUS |
| --- | --- | --- | --- | --- |
| BIRDS | TEIRESIAS | SATYR | EURYDICE | TRAGEDY |
| SOPHOCLES | HAIMON | FREE SPACE | ODES | DEATH |
| ANTISTROPHE | LOVE | ETEOCLES | SISTERS | EXODUS |
| PAEAN | BATTLE | HARMARTIA | EPISODE | PROLOGUE |

Antigone

| TRAGEDY | BURY | CATHARSIS | DEATH | PROLOGUE |
|---|---|---|---|---|
| PARADOS | ETHOS | HAIMON | TETRAOLOGY | EPISODE |
| CHORUS | SISTERS | FREE SPACE | DIONYSIA | THESPIS |
| EXODUS | ANTIGONE | GOD | PAEAN | LOGOS |
| ETEOCLES | SOUL | THEBES | LANGUAGE | REASON |

Antigone

| SOPHOCLES | OEDIPUS | CHORAGOS | PATHOS | ANTISTROPHE |
|---|---|---|---|---|
| SEAS | GOLD | MAN | ODES | LOVE |
| STROPHE | HUBRIS | FREE SPACE | BATTLE | HARMARTIA |
| CREON | EURYDICE | DIONYSOS | AESCHYLUS | ISMENE |
| TEIRESIAS | ZEUS | BIRDS | REASON | LANGUAGE |

Antigone

| DIONYSIA | LOVE | BIRDS | ETHOS | ZEUS |
| --- | --- | --- | --- | --- |
| HARMARTIA | SATYR | STROPHE | LOGOS | AESCHYLUS |
| PARADOS | CHORUS | FREE SPACE | SEAS | ISMENE |
| GOLD | TEIRESIAS | TETRAOLOGY | GOD | DEATH |
| TRAGEDY | BURY | HAIMON | CREON | THEBES |

Antigone

| ANTIGONE | CATHARSIS | PATHOS | MAN | REASON |
| --- | --- | --- | --- | --- |
| OEDIPUS | SOUL | PROLOGUE | PAEAN | HUBRIS |
| LANGUAGE | ETEOCLES | FREE SPACE | ANTISTROPHE | BATTLE |
| DIONYSOS | POLYNEICES | CHORAGOS | EPISODE | ODES |
| EXODUS | SISTERS | SOPHOCLES | THEBES | CREON |

Antigone

| BURY | EPISODE | TEIRESIAS | DEATH | BATTLE |
| --- | --- | --- | --- | --- |
| LANGUAGE | THESPIS | AESCHYLUS | THEBES | ANTISTROPHE |
| STROPHE | SOPHOCLES | FREE SPACE | OEDIPUS | REASON |
| TRAGEDY | DIONYSIA | CHORUS | GOD | CATHARSIS |
| PARADOS | PAEAN | ANTIGONE | CREON | HUBRIS |

Antigone

| HAIMON | ZEUS | PROLOGUE | EXODUS | TETRAOLOGY |
| --- | --- | --- | --- | --- |
| ETEOCLES | GOLD | LOVE | SEAS | SISTERS |
| POLYNEICES | EURYDICE | FREE SPACE | ETHOS | MAN |
| ODES | SOUL | ISMENE | CHORAGOS | LOGOS |
| BIRDS | DIONYSOS | HARMARTIA | HUBRIS | CREON |

Antigone

| THEBES | THESPIS | ISMENE | HUBRIS | DIONYSIA |
| --- | --- | --- | --- | --- |
| POLYNEICES | SATYR | TRAGEDY | AESCHYLUS | ETEOCLES |
| TEIRESIAS | CHORAGOS | FREE SPACE | EXODUS | SOUL |
| REASON | EURYDICE | SEAS | LOVE | TETRAOLOGY |
| HARMARTIA | HAIMON | PARADOS | PATHOS | EPISODE |

Antigone

| DEATH | GOD | PROLOGUE | STROPHE | OEDIPUS |
| --- | --- | --- | --- | --- |
| LOGOS | PAEAN | SISTERS | BIRDS | ANTIGONE |
| BURY | ODES | FREE SPACE | BATTLE | LANGUAGE |
| CATHARSIS | GOLD | CHORUS | DIONYSOS | ZEUS |
| MAN | CREON | SOPHOCLES | EPISODE | PATHOS |

Antigone

| DEATH | LOVE | CHORAGOS | BATTLE | CREON |
| --- | --- | --- | --- | --- |
| CHORUS | EURYDICE | CATHARSIS | SOUL | ZEUS |
| PAEAN | BIRDS | FREE SPACE | AESCHYLUS | GOD |
| LANGUAGE | DIONYSOS | HAIMON | ODES | PATHOS |
| SEAS | THESPIS | SOPHOCLES | THEBES | SISTERS |

Antigone

| TEIRESIAS | BURY | PARADOS | GOLD | TRAGEDY |
| --- | --- | --- | --- | --- |
| SATYR | STROPHE | EPISODE | TETRAOLOGY | LOGOS |
| MAN | POLYNEICES | FREE SPACE | ANTISTROPHE | HARMARTIA |
| DIONYSIA | HUBRIS | OEDIPUS | EXODUS | REASON |
| ETEOCLES | PROLOGUE | ANTIGONE | SISTERS | THEBES |

Antigone

| STROPHE | CREON | CHORAGOS | SOUL | MAN |
|---|---|---|---|---|
| PARADOS | HARMARTIA | SOPHOCLES | AESCHYLUS | EURYDICE |
| THEBES | EPISODE | FREE SPACE | PATHOS | ISMENE |
| DEATH | POLYNEICES | DIONYSOS | TETRAOLOGY | LOGOS |
| LOVE | REASON | DIONYSIA | GOLD | ZEUS |

Antigone

| TRAGEDY | HUBRIS | PAEAN | SATYR | BURY |
|---|---|---|---|---|
| GOD | EXODUS | SISTERS | HAIMON | PROLOGUE |
| BIRDS | CHORUS | FREE SPACE | BATTLE | LANGUAGE |
| SEAS | ETEOCLES | CATHARSIS | TEIRESIAS | ETHOS |
| OEDIPUS | ODES | ANTIGONE | ZEUS | GOLD |

Antigone

| LANGUAGE | HARMARTIA | GOLD | BURY | ZEUS |
|---|---|---|---|---|
| PARADOS | EPISODE | CHORUS | THESPIS | ANTISTROPHE |
| STROPHE | CATHARSIS | FREE SPACE | BIRDS | CREON |
| LOVE | HUBRIS | CHORAGOS | POLYNEICES | REASON |
| GOD | THEBES | SOUL | MAN | PATHOS |

Antigone

| ISMENE | SOPHOCLES | SISTERS | TRAGEDY | ETEOCLES |
|---|---|---|---|---|
| ETHOS | LOGOS | TETRAOLOGY | ANTIGONE | DIONYSOS |
| ODES | DIONYSIA | FREE SPACE | HAIMON | PAEAN |
| OEDIPUS | SEAS | SATYR | DEATH | EURYDICE |
| BATTLE | TEIRESIAS | AESCHYLUS | PATHOS | MAN |

Antigone

| SOUL | GOLD | ODES | STROPHE | LOGOS |
|---|---|---|---|---|
| THEBES | ZEUS | CHORAGOS | ETHOS | PATHOS |
| AESCHYLUS | BIRDS | FREE SPACE | ANTIGONE | DIONYSIA |
| ANTISTROPHE | ETEOCLES | HUBRIS | EPISODE | DEATH |
| EURYDICE | ISMENE | TETRAOLOGY | CREON | PARADOS |

Antigone

| REASON | CATHARSIS | SEAS | TRAGEDY | HARMARTIA |
|---|---|---|---|---|
| CHORUS | POLYNEICES | PAEAN | MAN | PROLOGUE |
| GOD | TEIRESIAS | FREE SPACE | EXODUS | THESPIS |
| DIONYSOS | BATTLE | BURY | SATYR | OEDIPUS |
| SISTERS | SOPHOCLES | LOVE | PARADOS | CREON |

Antigone

| AESCHYLUS | THEBES | HARMARTIA | EPISODE | SOUL |
|---|---|---|---|---|
| HAIMON | TETRAOLOGY | EURYDICE | PROLOGUE | TEIRESIAS |
| ODES | GOD | FREE SPACE | REASON | BATTLE |
| PARADOS | POLYNEICES | SOPHOCLES | ETHOS | LOGOS |
| ZEUS | OEDIPUS | SEAS | DEATH | DIONYSOS |

Antigone

| CHORUS | LANGUAGE | CHORAGOS | STROPHE | MAN |
|---|---|---|---|---|
| THESPIS | GOLD | CREON | CATHARSIS | SATYR |
| ISMENE | DIONYSIA | FREE SPACE | ANTISTROPHE | HUBRIS |
| SISTERS | LOVE | EXODUS | BURY | PAEAN |
| ETEOCLES | PATHOS | TRAGEDY | DIONYSOS | DEATH |

Antigone

| DEATH | EURYDICE | TEIRESIAS | DIONYSOS | CATHARSIS |
|---|---|---|---|---|
| SOPHOCLES | OEDIPUS | HUBRIS | SISTERS | SOUL |
| PARADOS | BURY | FREE SPACE | TETRAOLOGY | LOGOS |
| ISMENE | HAIMON | REASON | SEAS | EXODUS |
| CHORAGOS | PAEAN | PATHOS | MAN | ANTISTROPHE |

Antigone

| ODES | STROPHE | BATTLE | ETEOCLES | GOLD |
|---|---|---|---|---|
| BIRDS | ETHOS | EPISODE | CHORUS | AESCHYLUS |
| HARMARTIA | LOVE | FREE SPACE | THESPIS | TRAGEDY |
| GOD | ZEUS | CREON | ANTIGONE | DIONYSIA |
| LANGUAGE | THEBES | PROLOGUE | ANTISTROPHE | MAN |

Antigone

| LOGOS | TRAGEDY | AESCHYLUS | ZEUS | PATHOS |
| --- | --- | --- | --- | --- |
| MAN | HAIMON | REASON | THESPIS | HUBRIS |
| BATTLE | DIONYSOS | FREE SPACE | ETHOS | GOD |
| PROLOGUE | CHORUS | LANGUAGE | SISTERS | HARMARTIA |
| DIONYSIA | ANTISTROPHE | LOVE | EPISODE | GOLD |

Antigone

| THEBES | BURY | DEATH | OEDIPUS | POLYNEICES |
| --- | --- | --- | --- | --- |
| PARADOS | EXODUS | ISMENE | SOPHOCLES | TETRAOLOGY |
| EURYDICE | SOUL | FREE SPACE | CHORAGOS | SEAS |
| CATHARSIS | STROPHE | ETEOCLES | BIRDS | ANTIGONE |
| PAEAN | ODES | TEIRESIAS | GOLD | EPISODE |

Antigone

| GOD | LANGUAGE | HAIMON | OEDIPUS | CATHARSIS |
| --- | --- | --- | --- | --- |
| GOLD | SOPHOCLES | HARMARTIA | PATHOS | POLYNEICES |
| BURY | SOUL | FREE SPACE | LOGOS | CHORUS |
| CHORAGOS | ISMENE | REASON | STROPHE | ODES |
| SATYR | EPISODE | CREON | PROLOGUE | PARADOS |

Antigone

| ETHOS | THESPIS | HUBRIS | AESCHYLUS | DIONYSOS |
| --- | --- | --- | --- | --- |
| EXODUS | SISTERS | TRAGEDY | BATTLE | ANTISTROPHE |
| TETRAOLOGY | SEAS | FREE SPACE | DEATH | THEBES |
| TEIRESIAS | ANTIGONE | MAN | PAEAN | ZEUS |
| EURYDICE | LOVE | DIONYSIA | PARADOS | PROLOGUE |

Antigone

| MAN | LOGOS | TEIRESIAS | PARADOS | ETHOS |
|---|---|---|---|---|
| ZEUS | BATTLE | HARMARTIA | ANTISTROPHE | CHORUS |
| PAEAN | HAIMON | FREE SPACE | BURY | PROLOGUE |
| THEBES | ANTIGONE | PATHOS | EURYDICE | SOUL |
| LANGUAGE | CREON | DIONYSIA | EXODUS | OEDIPUS |

Antigone

| ISMENE | EPISODE | SATYR | AESCHYLUS | REASON |
|---|---|---|---|---|
| POLYNEICES | BIRDS | GOD | SEAS | TRAGEDY |
| ODES | CHORAGOS | FREE SPACE | LOVE | HUBRIS |
| CATHARSIS | GOLD | STROPHE | SISTERS | ETEOCLES |
| DEATH | TETRAOLOGY | DIONYSOS | OEDIPUS | EXODUS |

Antigone

| ETHOS | HARMARTIA | PATHOS | HUBRIS | BIRDS |
|---|---|---|---|---|
| ODES | STROPHE | REASON | LANGUAGE | ANTISTROPHE |
| SOUL | BATTLE | FREE SPACE | ETEOCLES | GOLD |
| ISMENE | DIONYSIA | AESCHYLUS | CHORAGOS | EURYDICE |
| PAEAN | THESPIS | EXODUS | HAIMON | THEBES |

Antigone

| OEDIPUS | SOPHOCLES | LOVE | POLYNEICES | ANTIGONE |
|---|---|---|---|---|
| DIONYSOS | CREON | CHORUS | PARADOS | LOGOS |
| TRAGEDY | ZEUS | FREE SPACE | SISTERS | TETRAOLOGY |
| GOD | BURY | EPISODE | CATHARSIS | DEATH |
| TEIRESIAS | SATYR | PROLOGUE | THEBES | HAIMON |

# Antigone Vocabulary Word List

| No. | Word | Clue/Definition |
|---|---|---|
| 1. | ANARCHISTS | Those who reject all forms of coercive control and authority |
| 2. | APHORISM | Tersely phrased statement of a truth or opinion; an adage |
| 3. | ASTRAY | Away from the right or good; straying to or into wrong or evil ways |
| 4. | AUGURY | Art, ability, or practice of making predictions |
| 5. | AUSPICIOUS | Attended by favorable circumstances |
| 6. | BARBARIC | Without civilizing influences |
| 7. | BARROW | Large mound of earth or stones placed over a burial site |
| 8. | BLASPHEMY | Profane act, utterance, or writing concerning God |
| 9. | BRAWL | Noisy quarrel or fight |
| 10. | BRAY | Loud, harsh sound resembling that of a donkey |
| 11. | BRAZEN | Made of brass |
| 12. | CALAMITY | Event that brings terrible loss; disaster |
| 13. | CARRION | Feeding on dead and decaying flesh |
| 14. | CITADEL | Fortress in a commanding position in or near a city |
| 15. | CLEMENT | Inclined to be lenient or merciful |
| 16. | COMPREHENSIVE | Marked by or showing extensive understanding |
| 17. | COMPULSIVE | Having the capacity to exert a strong, irresistible influence on |
| 18. | CONSIDER | Think carefully about |
| 19. | CONTEMPT | Feeling or attitude of regarding someone or something as inferior |
| 20. | DECREE | Authoritative order having the force of law |
| 21. | DEFERENCE | Yielding to the opinion, wishes, or judgment of another |
| 22. | DEFLECTS | Turns aside or causes to turn aside |
| 23. | DEFY | Refuse to submit to or cooperate with |
| 24. | DEMORALIZING | Undermining the confidence or morale of; dishearten |
| 25. | DIRGES | Funeral hymns |
| 26. | DIVINERS | Those who can predict the future |
| 27. | DROWSE | To be half asleep |
| 28. | EDDY | Current of water moving against the direction of the main current |
| 29. | EDICT | Formal command |
| 30. | EMBERS | Small, glowing pieces of coal or wood, as in a dying fire |
| 31. | ENDURED | Bore with tolerance |
| 32. | ENTRAILS | Internal organs, especially the intestines |
| 33. | FOLLY | Lack of good sense, understanding, or foresight |
| 34. | GALES | Very strong winds |
| 35. | GLUT | Fill beyond capacity, especially with food |
| 36. | IMPLACABLE | Impossible to placate or appease |
| 37. | INSOLENCE | Rudeness or disrespect |
| 38. | LAMENTATION | Cry of sorrow and grief |
| 39. | LITHE | Marked by effortless grace |
| 40. | MARSHAL | Military officer of the highest rank in some countries |
| 41. | PERVERSE | Obstinately persisting in an error or fault; wrongly self-willed or stubborn |
| 42. | PIETY | Quality of being pious or reverent |
| 43. | PREVAIL | To be greater in strength or influence; triumph |
| 44. | PROCLAMATION | Official, formal, public announcement |
| 45. | PROW | Forward part of a ship's hull |
| 46. | ROUSED | Excited, as to anger or action; stirred up |
| 47. | SATED | Satisfied to excess |
| 48. | SENTRIES | Guards, especially soldiers posted at a given spot to prevent the passage of unauthorized persons |
| 49. | SLACKEN | Make or become less tense, taut, or firm; loosen |

**Antigone Vocabulary Word List**

| No. | Word | Clue/Definition |
|---|---|---|
| 50. | SUBORDINATE | Subject to the authority or control of another |
| 51. | SULTRY | Very humid and hot |
| 52. | TORMENTED | Caused great physical pain or mental anguish |
| 53. | TRANSCENDS | Passes beyond the limits of something |
| 54. | TRANSGRESS | Commit an offense by violating a law or command; sin |
| 55. | VENGEANCE | Infliction of punishment in return for a wrong committed |
| 56. | VIGIL | Watch kept during normal sleeping hours |
| 57. | VILE | Deserving of contempt or scorn |
| 58. | WRETCHED | In a deplorable state of distress or misfortune |
| 59. | YIELD | Give up (an advantage, for example) to another; concede |

Antigone Vocabulary Fill In The Blanks 1

_____ 1. Military officer of the highest rank in some countries

_____ 2. Official, formal, public announcement

_____ 3. Large mound of earth or stones placed over a burial site

_____ 4. Small, glowing pieces of coal or wood, as in a dying fire

_____ 5. In a deplorable state of distress or misfortune

_____ 6. Impossible to placate or appease

_____ 7. Tersely phrased statement of a truth or opinion; an adage

_____ 8. To be half asleep

_____ 9. Passes beyond the limits of something

_____ 10. Forward part of a ship's hull

_____ 11. Without civilizing influences

_____ 12. Cry of sorrow and grief

_____ 13. Subject to the authority or control of another

_____ 14. Made of brass

_____ 15. Feeling or attitude of regarding someone or something as inferior

_____ 16. Quality of being pious or reverent

_____ 17. Give up (an advantage, for example) to another; concede

_____ 18. Marked by or showing extensive understanding

_____ 19. Having the capacity to exert a strong, irresistible influence on

_____ 20. Fill beyond capacity, especially with food

Antigone Vocabulary Fill In The Blanks 1 Answer Key

| | |
|---|---|
| MARSHAL | 1. Military officer of the highest rank in some countries |
| PROCLAMATION | 2. Official, formal, public announcement |
| BARROW | 3. Large mound of earth or stones placed over a burial site |
| EMBERS | 4. Small, glowing pieces of coal or wood, as in a dying fire |
| WRETCHED | 5. In a deplorable state of distress or misfortune |
| IMPLACABLE | 6. Impossible to placate or appease |
| APHORISM | 7. Tersely phrased statement of a truth or opinion; an adage |
| DROWSE | 8. To be half asleep |
| TRANSCENDS | 9. Passes beyond the limits of something |
| PROW | 10. Forward part of a ship's hull |
| BARBARIC | 11. Without civilizing influences |
| LAMENTATION | 12. Cry of sorrow and grief |
| SUBORDINATE | 13. Subject to the authority or control of another |
| BRAZEN | 14. Made of brass |
| CONTEMPT | 15. Feeling or attitude of regarding someone or something as inferior |
| PIETY | 16. Quality of being pious or reverent |
| YIELD | 17. Give up (an advantage, for example) to another; concede |
| COMPREHENSIVE | 18. Marked by or showing extensive understanding |
| COMPULSIVE | 19. Having the capacity to exert a strong, irresistible influence on |
| GLUT | 20. Fill beyond capacity, especially with food |

Antigone Vocabulary Fill In The Blanks 2

_____ 1. Quality of being pious or reverent

_____ 2. Loud, harsh sound resembling that of a donkey

_____ 3. Passes beyond the limits of something

_____ 4. Guards, especially soldiers posted at a given spot to prevent the passage of unauthorized persons

_____ 5. Excited, as to anger or action; stirred up

_____ 6. Attended by favorable circumstances

_____ 7. Think carefully about

_____ 8. Refuse to submit to or cooperate with

_____ 9. Caused great physical pain or mental anguish

_____ 10. Satisfied to excess

_____ 11. Very humid and hot

_____ 12. Official, formal, public announcement

_____ 13. To be greater in strength or influence; triumph

_____ 14. Noisy quarrel or fight

_____ 15. Obstinately persisting in an error or fault; wrongly self-willed or stubborn

_____ 16. Internal organs, especially the intestines

_____ 17. Feeling or attitude of regarding someone or something as inferior

_____ 18. Deserving of contempt or scorn

_____ 19. Marked by or showing extensive understanding

_____ 20. Impossible to placate or appease

Antigone Vocabulary Fill In The Blanks 2 Answer Key

| | |
|---|---|
| PIETY | 1. Quality of being pious or reverent |
| BRAY | 2. Loud, harsh sound resembling that of a donkey |
| TRANSCENDS | 3. Passes beyond the limits of something |
| SENTRIES | 4. Guards, especially soldiers posted at a given spot to prevent the passage of unauthorized persons |
| ROUSED | 5. Excited, as to anger or action; stirred up |
| AUSPICIOUS | 6. Attended by favorable circumstances |
| CONSIDER | 7. Think carefully about |
| DEFY | 8. Refuse to submit to or cooperate with |
| TORMENTED | 9. Caused great physical pain or mental anguish |
| SATED | 10. Satisfied to excess |
| SULTRY | 11. Very humid and hot |
| PROCLAMATION | 12. Official, formal, public announcement |
| PREVAIL | 13. To be greater in strength or influence; triumph |
| BRAWL | 14. Noisy quarrel or fight |
| PERVERSE | 15. Obstinately persisting in an error or fault; wrongly self-willed or stubborn |
| ENTRAILS | 16. Internal organs, especially the intestines |
| CONTEMPT | 17. Feeling or attitude of regarding someone or something as inferior |
| VILE | 18. Deserving of contempt or scorn |
| COMPREHENSIVE | 19. Marked by or showing extensive understanding |
| IMPLACABLE | 20. Impossible to placate or appease |

Antigone Vocabulary Fill In The Blanks 3

_____ 1. Having the capacity to exert a strong, irresistible influence on

_____ 2. Official, formal, public announcement

_____ 3. To be half asleep

_____ 4. Attended by favorable circumstances

_____ 5. Event that brings terrible loss; disaster

_____ 6. Those who reject all forms of coercive control and authority

_____ 7. Feeding on dead and decaying flesh

_____ 8. Excited, as to anger or action; stirred up

_____ 9. Passes beyond the limits of something

_____ 10. Away from the right or good; straying to or into wrong or evil ways

_____ 11. Without civilizing influences

_____ 12. Noisy quarrel or fight

_____ 13. Quality of being pious or reverent

_____ 14. Forward part of a ship's hull

_____ 15. Fortress in a commanding position in or near a city

_____ 16. Formal command

_____ 17. Refuse to submit to or cooperate with

_____ 18. Impossible to placate or appease

_____ 19. Authoritative order having the force of law

_____ 20. Cry of sorrow and grief

Antigone Vocabulary Fill In The Blanks 3 Answer Key

| | |
|---|---|
| COMPULSIVE | 1. Having the capacity to exert a strong, irresistible influence on |
| PROCLAMATION | 2. Official, formal, public announcement |
| DROWSE | 3. To be half asleep |
| AUSPICIOUS | 4. Attended by favorable circumstances |
| CALAMITY | 5. Event that brings terrible loss; disaster |
| ANARCHISTS | 6. Those who reject all forms of coercive control and authority |
| CARRION | 7. Feeding on dead and decaying flesh |
| ROUSED | 8. Excited, as to anger or action; stirred up |
| TRANSCENDS | 9. Passes beyond the limits of something |
| ASTRAY | 10. Away from the right or good; straying to or into wrong or evil ways |
| BARBARIC | 11. Without civilizing influences |
| BRAWL | 12. Noisy quarrel or fight |
| PIETY | 13. Quality of being pious or reverent |
| PROW | 14. Forward part of a ship's hull |
| CITADEL | 15. Fortress in a commanding position in or near a city |
| EDICT | 16. Formal command |
| DEFY | 17. Refuse to submit to or cooperate with |
| IMPLACABLE | 18. Impossible to placate or appease |
| DECREE | 19. Authoritative order having the force of law |
| LAMENTATION | 20. Cry of sorrow and grief |

Antigone Vocabulary Fill In The Blanks 4

_____ 1. Small, glowing pieces of coal or wood, as in a dying fire

_____ 2. Those who reject all forms of coercive control and authority

_____ 3. Art, ability, or practice of making predictions

_____ 4. Obstinately persisting in an error or fault; wrongly self-willed or stubborn

_____ 5. Loud, harsh sound resembling that of a donkey

_____ 6. Inclined to be lenient or merciful

_____ 7. Very strong winds

_____ 8. Made of brass

_____ 9. Large mound of earth or stones placed over a burial site

_____ 10. Lack of good sense, understanding, or foresight

_____ 11. Those who can predict the future

_____ 12. Having the capacity to exert a strong, irresistible influence on

_____ 13. Cry of sorrow and grief

_____ 14. Military officer of the highest rank in some countries

_____ 15. Internal organs, especially the intestines

_____ 16. Subject to the authority or control of another

_____ 17. Away from the right or good; straying to or into wrong or evil ways

_____ 18. Marked by effortless grace

_____ 19. Excited, as to anger or action; stirred up

_____ 20. Attended by favorable circumstances

Antigone Vocabulary Fill In The Blanks 4 Answer Key

| | |
|---|---|
| EMBERS | 1. Small, glowing pieces of coal or wood, as in a dying fire |
| ANARCHISTS | 2. Those who reject all forms of coercive control and authority |
| AUGURY | 3. Art, ability, or practice of making predictions |
| PERVERSE | 4. Obstinately persisting in an error or fault; wrongly self-willed or stubborn |
| BRAY | 5. Loud, harsh sound resembling that of a donkey |
| CLEMENT | 6. Inclined to be lenient or merciful |
| GALES | 7. Very strong winds |
| BRAZEN | 8. Made of brass |
| BARROW | 9. Large mound of earth or stones placed over a burial site |
| FOLLY | 10. Lack of good sense, understanding, or foresight |
| DIVINERS | 11. Those who can predict the future |
| COMPULSIVE | 12. Having the capacity to exert a strong, irresistible influence on |
| LAMENTATION | 13. Cry of sorrow and grief |
| MARSHAL | 14. Military officer of the highest rank in some countries |
| ENTRAILS | 15. Internal organs, especially the intestines |
| SUBORDINATE | 16. Subject to the authority or control of another |
| ASTRAY | 17. Away from the right or good; straying to or into wrong or evil ways |
| LITHE | 18. Marked by effortless grace |
| ROUSED | 19. Excited, as to anger or action; stirred up |
| AUSPICIOUS | 20. Attended by favorable circumstances |

Antigone Vocabulary Matching 1

___ 1. SENTRIES  A. Give up (an advantage, for example) to another; concede
___ 2. PREVAIL  B. Event that brings terrible loss; disaster
___ 3. SLACKEN  C. To be half asleep
___ 4. SATED  D. Profane act, utterance, or writing concerning God
___ 5. GLUT  E. Without civilizing influences
___ 6. CLEMENT  F. Official, formal, public announcement
___ 7. TORMENTED  G. Quality of being pious or reverent
___ 8. CONTEMPT  H. Attended by favorable circumstances
___ 9. CALAMITY  I. Those who reject all forms of coercive control and authority
___ 10. PROCLAMATION  J. Refuse to submit to or cooperate with
___ 11. ENTRAILS  K. Satisfied to excess
___ 12. BARBARIC  L. Lack of good sense, understanding, or foresight
___ 13. BLASPHEMY  M. Guards, especially soldiers posted at a given spot to prevent the passage of unauthorized persons
___ 14. AUSPICIOUS  N. Caused great physical pain or mental anguish
___ 15. PIETY  O. Commit an offense by violating a law or command; sin
___ 16. ANARCHISTS  P. To be greater in strength or influence; triumph
___ 17. DROWSE  Q. Away from the right or good; straying to or into wrong or evil ways
___ 18. WRETCHED  R. Feeling or attitude of regarding someone or something as inferior
___ 19. DEFERENCE  S. Internal organs, especially the intestines
___ 20. ASTRAY  T. Fill beyond capacity, especially with food
___ 21. TRANSGRESS  U. Make or become less tense, taut, or firm; loosen
___ 22. DEFY  V. In a deplorable state of distress or misfortune
___ 23. DEFLECTS  W. Turns aside or causes to turn aside
___ 24. YIELD  X. Yielding to the opinion, wishes, or judgment of another
___ 25. FOLLY  Y. Inclined to be lenient or merciful

Antigone Vocabulary Matching 1 Answer Key

| | | |
|---|---|---|
| M - 1. | SENTRIES | A. Give up (an advantage, for example) to another; concede |
| P - 2. | PREVAIL | B. Event that brings terrible loss; disaster |
| U - 3. | SLACKEN | C. To be half asleep |
| K - 4. | SATED | D. Profane act, utterance, or writing concerning God |
| T - 5. | GLUT | E. Without civilizing influences |
| Y - 6. | CLEMENT | F. Official, formal, public announcement |
| N - 7. | TORMENTED | G. Quality of being pious or reverent |
| R - 8. | CONTEMPT | H. Attended by favorable circumstances |
| B - 9. | CALAMITY | I. Those who reject all forms of coercive control and authority |
| F - 10. | PROCLAMATION | J. Refuse to submit to or cooperate with |
| S - 11. | ENTRAILS | K. Satisfied to excess |
| E - 12. | BARBARIC | L. Lack of good sense, understanding, or foresight |
| D - 13. | BLASPHEMY | M. Guards, especially soldiers posted at a given spot to prevent the passage of unauthorized persons |
| H - 14. | AUSPICIOUS | N. Caused great physical pain or mental anguish |
| G - 15. | PIETY | O. Commit an offense by violating a law or command; sin |
| I - 16. | ANARCHISTS | P. To be greater in strength or influence; triumph |
| C - 17. | DROWSE | Q. Away from the right or good; straying to or into wrong or evil ways |
| V - 18. | WRETCHED | R. Feeling or attitude of regarding someone or something as inferior |
| X - 19. | DEFERENCE | S. Internal organs, especially the intestines |
| Q - 20. | ASTRAY | T. Fill beyond capacity, especially with food |
| O - 21. | TRANSGRESS | U. Make or become less tense, taut, or firm; loosen |
| J - 22. | DEFY | V. In a deplorable state of distress or misfortune |
| W - 23. | DEFLECTS | W. Turns aside or causes to turn aside |
| A - 24. | YIELD | X. Yielding to the opinion, wishes, or judgment of another |
| L - 25. | FOLLY | Y. Inclined to be lenient or merciful |

Antigone Vocabulary Matching 2

___ 1. ASTRAY          A. Bore with tolerance
___ 2. DROWSE          B. To be greater in strength or influence; triumph
___ 3. BARBARIC        C. Feeling or attitude of regarding someone or something as inferior
___ 4. ANARCHISTS      D. Internal organs, especially the intestines
___ 5. DEMORALIZING    E. Without civilizing influences
___ 6. ENTRAILS        F. Formal command
___ 7. VENGEANCE       G. Away from the right or good; straying to or into wrong or evil ways
___ 8. EDDY            H. Military officer of the highest rank in some countries
___ 9. DECREE          I. Very humid and hot
___10. BLASPHEMY       J. Infliction of punishment in return for a wrong committed
___11. SULTRY          K. Satisfied to excess
___12. CITADEL         L. To be half asleep
___13. VILE            M. Think carefully about
___14. CONTEMPT        N. In a deplorable state of distress or misfortune
___15. ENDURED         O. Profane act, utterance, or writing concerning God
___16. MARSHAL         P. Current of water moving against the direction of the main current
___17. CONSIDER        Q. Deserving of contempt or scorn
___18. PROCLAMATION    R. Turns aside or causes to turn aside
___19. EDICT           S. Authoritative order having the force of law
___20. WRETCHED        T. Those who reject all forms of coercive control and authority
___21. SATED           U. Fortress in a commanding position in or near a city
___22. PREVAIL         V. Official, formal, public announcement
___23. TRANSGRESS      W. Commit an offense by violating a law or command; sin
___24. DEFLECTS        X. Fill beyond capacity, especially with food
___25. GLUT            Y. Undermining the confidence or morale of; dishearten

Antigone Vocabulary Matching 2 Answer Key

| | | |
|---|---|---|
| G - 1. ASTRAY | A. | Bore with tolerance |
| L - 2. DROWSE | B. | To be greater in strength or influence; triumph |
| E - 3. BARBARIC | C. | Feeling or attitude of regarding someone or something as inferior |
| T - 4. ANARCHISTS | D. | Internal organs, especially the intestines |
| Y - 5. DEMORALIZING | E. | Without civilizing influences |
| D - 6. ENTRAILS | F. | Formal command |
| J - 7. VENGEANCE | G. | Away from the right or good; straying to or into wrong or evil ways |
| P - 8. EDDY | H. | Military officer of the highest rank in some countries |
| S - 9. DECREE | I. | Very humid and hot |
| O -10. BLASPHEMY | J. | Infliction of punishment in return for a wrong committed |
| I - 11. SULTRY | K. | Satisfied to excess |
| U -12. CITADEL | L. | To be half asleep |
| Q -13. VILE | M. | Think carefully about |
| C -14. CONTEMPT | N. | In a deplorable state of distress or misfortune |
| A -15. ENDURED | O. | Profane act, utterance, or writing concerning God |
| H -16. MARSHAL | P. | Current of water moving against the direction of the main current |
| M -17. CONSIDER | Q. | Deserving of contempt or scorn |
| V -18. PROCLAMATION | R. | Turns aside or causes to turn aside |
| F -19. EDICT | S. | Authoritative order having the force of law |
| N -20. WRETCHED | T. | Those who reject all forms of coercive control and authority |
| K -21. SATED | U. | Fortress in a commanding position in or near a city |
| B -22. PREVAIL | V. | Official, formal, public announcement |
| W -23. TRANSGRESS | W. | Commit an offense by violating a law or command; sin |
| R -24. DEFLECTS | X. | Fill beyond capacity, especially with food |
| X -25. GLUT | Y. | Undermining the confidence or morale of; dishearten |

Antigone Vocabulary Matching 3

___ 1. CONSIDER            A. Feeding on dead and decaying flesh
___ 2. YIELD               B. Without civilizing influences
___ 3. COMPREHENSIVE       C. Made of brass
___ 4. WRETCHED            D. Authoritative order having the force of law
___ 5. DEMORALIZING        E. Tersely phrased statement of a truth or opinion; an adage
___ 6. LAMENTATION         F. Very strong winds
___ 7. GALES               G. Infliction of punishment in return for a wrong committed
___ 8. CARRION             H. Give up (an advantage, for example) to another; concede
___ 9. SUBORDINATE         I. Satisfied to excess
___10. EDICT               J. Lack of good sense, understanding, or foresight
___11. TRANSCENDS          K. Marked by effortless grace
___12. BRAWL               L. Away from the right or good; straying to or into wrong or evil ways
___13. BARBARIC            M. Formal command
___14. ROUSED              N. Military officer of the highest rank in some countries
___15. MARSHAL             O. Noisy quarrel or fight
___16. TORMENTED           P. Think carefully about
___17. SATED               Q. Subject to the authority or control of another
___18. LITHE               R. Caused great physical pain or mental anguish
___19. SENTRIES            S. Undermining the confidence or morale of; dishearten
___20. FOLLY               T. Excited, as to anger or action; stirred up
___21. BRAZEN              U. Guards, especially soldiers posted at a given spot to prevent the passage of unauthorized persons
___22. ASTRAY              V. Marked by or showing extensive understanding
___23. DECREE              W. In a deplorable state of distress or misfortune
___24. VENGEANCE           X. Passes beyond the limits of something
___25. APHORISM            Y. Cry of sorrow and grief

Antigone Vocabulary Matching 3 Answer Key

| | | |
|---|---|---|
| P - 1. | CONSIDER | A. Feeding on dead and decaying flesh |
| H - 2. | YIELD | B. Without civilizing influences |
| V - 3. | COMPREHENSIVE | C. Made of brass |
| W - 4. | WRETCHED | D. Authoritative order having the force of law |
| S - 5. | DEMORALIZING | E. Tersely phrased statement of a truth or opinion; an adage |
| Y - 6. | LAMENTATION | F. Very strong winds |
| F - 7. | GALES | G. Infliction of punishment in return for a wrong committed |
| A - 8. | CARRION | H. Give up (an advantage, for example) to another; concede |
| Q - 9. | SUBORDINATE | I. Satisfied to excess |
| M - 10. | EDICT | J. Lack of good sense, understanding, or foresight |
| X - 11. | TRANSCENDS | K. Marked by effortless grace |
| O - 12. | BRAWL | L. Away from the right or good; straying to or into wrong or evil ways |
| B - 13. | BARBARIC | M. Formal command |
| T - 14. | ROUSED | N. Military officer of the highest rank in some countries |
| N - 15. | MARSHAL | O. Noisy quarrel or fight |
| R - 16. | TORMENTED | P. Think carefully about |
| I - 17. | SATED | Q. Subject to the authority or control of another |
| K - 18. | LITHE | R. Caused great physical pain or mental anguish |
| U - 19. | SENTRIES | S. Undermining the confidence or morale of; dishearten |
| J - 20. | FOLLY | T. Excited, as to anger or action; stirred up |
| C - 21. | BRAZEN | U. Guards, especially soldiers posted at a given spot to prevent the passage of unauthorized persons |
| L - 22. | ASTRAY | V. Marked by or showing extensive understanding |
| D - 23. | DECREE | W. In a deplorable state of distress or misfortune |
| G - 24. | VENGEANCE | X. Passes beyond the limits of something |
| E - 25. | APHORISM | Y. Cry of sorrow and grief |

Antigone Vocabulary Matching 4

___ 1. INSOLENCE           A. Event that brings terrible loss; disaster
___ 2. MARSHAL             B. Very humid and hot
___ 3. ENDURED             C. Passes beyond the limits of something
___ 4. PIETY               D. Official, formal, public announcement
___ 5. ANARCHISTS          E. Military officer of the highest rank in some countries
___ 6. BARBARIC            F. Watch kept during normal sleeping hours
___ 7. PROCLAMATION        G. Art, ability, or practice of making predictions
___ 8. TRANSGRESS          H. Rudeness or disrespect
___ 9. TRANSCENDS          I. Those who reject all forms of coercive control and authority
___10. EDDY                J. Fortress in a commanding position in or near a city
___11. CALAMITY            K. Quality of being pious or reverent
___12. GALES               L. Current of water moving against the direction of the main current
___13. SULTRY              M. Impossible to placate or appease
___14. DIRGES              N. Refuse to submit to or cooperate with
___15. DEFY                O. Commit an offense by violating a law or command; sin
___16. AUGURY              P. Marked by or showing extensive understanding
___17. CITADEL             Q. Make or become less tense, taut, or firm; loosen
___18. VIGIL               R. Lack of good sense, understanding, or foresight
___19. FOLLY               S. Without civilizing influences
___20. CONSIDER            T. Profane act, utterance, or writing concerning God
___21. SENTRIES            U. Bore with tolerance
___22. COMPREHENSIVE       V. Very strong winds
___23. IMPLACABLE          W. Guards, especially soldiers posted at a given spot to prevent the passage of unauthorized persons
___24. SLACKEN             X. Think carefully about
___25. BLASPHEMY           Y. Funeral hymns

Antigone Vocabulary Matching 4 Answer Key

H - 1. INSOLENCE
E - 2. MARSHAL
U - 3. ENDURED
K - 4. PIETY
I - 5. ANARCHISTS
S - 6. BARBARIC
D - 7. PROCLAMATION
O - 8. TRANSGRESS
C - 9. TRANSCENDS
L - 10. EDDY
A - 11. CALAMITY
V - 12. GALES
B - 13. SULTRY
Y - 14. DIRGES
N - 15. DEFY
G - 16. AUGURY
J - 17. CITADEL
F - 18. VIGIL
R - 19. FOLLY
X - 20. CONSIDER
W - 21. SENTRIES
P - 22. COMPREHENSIVE
M - 23. IMPLACABLE
Q - 24. SLACKEN
T - 25. BLASPHEMY

A. Event that brings terrible loss; disaster
B. Very humid and hot
C. Passes beyond the limits of something
D. Official, formal, public announcement
E. Military officer of the highest rank in some countries
F. Watch kept during normal sleeping hours
G. Art, ability, or practice of making predictions
H. Rudeness or disrespect
I. Those who reject all forms of coercive control and authority
J. Fortress in a commanding position in or near a city
K. Quality of being pious or reverent
L. Current of water moving against the direction of the main current
M. Impossible to placate or appease
N. Refuse to submit to or cooperate with
O. Commit an offense by violating a law or command; sin
P. Marked by or showing extensive understanding
Q. Make or become less tense, taut, or firm; loosen
R. Lack of good sense, understanding, or foresight
S. Without civilizing influences
T. Profane act, utterance, or writing concerning God
U. Bore with tolerance
V. Very strong winds
W. Guards, especially soldiers posted at a given spot to prevent the passage of unauthorized persons
X. Think carefully about
Y. Funeral hymns

Antigone Vocabulary Magic Squares 1

Match the definition with the vocabulary word. Put your answers in the magic squares below. When your answers are correct, all columns and rows will add to the same number.

A. TRANSCENDS
B. VENGEANCE
C. SATED
D. DECREE
E. SUBORDINATE
F. EDDY
G. VIGIL
H. LAMENTATION
I. CITADEL
J. PERVERSE
K. AUGURY
L. ENTRAILS
M. SENTRIES
N. INSOLENCE
O. CARRION
P. CALAMITY

1. Infliction of punishment in return for a wrong committed
2. Watch kept during normal sleeping hours
3. Art, ability, or practice of making predictions
4. Rudeness or disrespect
5. Guards, especially soldiers posted at a given spot to prevent the passage of unauthorized persons
6. Internal organs, especially the intestines
7. Cry of sorrow and grief
8. Passes beyond the limits of something
9. Event that brings terrible loss; disaster
10. Fortress in a commanding position in or near a city
11. Subject to the authority or control of another
12. Authoritative order having the force of law
13. Satisfied to excess
14. Current of water moving against the direction of the main current
15. Obstinately persisting in an error or fault; wrongly self-willed or stubborn
16. Feeding on dead and decaying flesh

| A= | B= | C= | D= |
| --- | --- | --- | --- |
| E= | F= | G= | H= |
| I= | J= | K= | L= |
| M= | N= | O= | P= |

Antigone Vocabulary Magic Squares 1 Answer Key

Match the definition with the vocabulary word. Put your answers in the magic squares below. When your answers are correct, all columns and rows will add to the same number.

A. TRANSCENDS
B. VENGEANCE
C. SATED
D. DECREE
E. SUBORDINATE
F. EDDY
G. VIGIL
H. LAMENTATION
I. CITADEL
J. PERVERSE
K. AUGURY
L. ENTRAILS
M. SENTRIES
N. INSOLENCE
O. CARRION
P. CALAMITY

1. Infliction of punishment in return for a wrong committed
2. Watch kept during normal sleeping hours
3. Art, ability, or practice of making predictions
4. Rudeness or disrespect
5. Guards, especially soldiers posted at a given spot to prevent the passage of unauthorized persons
6. Internal organs, especially the intestines
7. Cry of sorrow and grief
8. Passes beyond the limits of something
9. Event that brings terrible loss; disaster
10. Fortress in a commanding position in or near a city
11. Subject to the authority or control of another
12. Authoritative order having the force of law
13. Satisfied to excess
14. Current of water moving against the direction of the main current
15. Obstinately persisting in an error or fault; wrongly self-willed or stubborn
16. Feeding on dead and decaying flesh

| A=8 | B=1 | C=13 | D=12 |
| E=11 | F=14 | G=2 | H=7 |
| I=10 | J=15 | K=3 | L=6 |
| M=5 | N=4 | O=16 | P=9 |

Antigone Vocabulary Magic Squares 2

Match the definition with the vocabulary word. Put your answers in the magic squares below. When your answers are correct, all columns and rows will add to the same number.

A. BRAWL
B. CITADEL
C. CLEMENT
D. INSOLENCE
E. CONTEMPT
F. DIVINERS
G. GALES
H. SATED
I. AUSPICIOUS
J. BARROW
K. BRAY
L. TORMENTED
M. BLASPHEMY
N. CONSIDER
O. ENDURED
P. EMBERS

1. Inclined to be lenient or merciful
2. Large mound of earth or stones placed over a burial site
3. Those who can predict the future
4. Bore with tolerance
5. Small, glowing pieces of coal or wood, as in a dying fire
6. Feeling or attitude of regarding someone or something as inferior
7. Attended by favorable circumstances
8. Rudeness or disrespect
9. Profane act, utterance, or writing concerning God
10. Satisfied to excess
11. Caused great physical pain or mental anguish
12. Noisy quarrel or fight
13. Fortress in a commanding position in or near a city
14. Loud, harsh sound resembling that of a donkey
15. Very strong winds
16. Think carefully about

| A= | B= | C= | D= |
| E= | F= | G= | H= |
| I= | J= | K= | L= |
| M= | N= | O= | P= |

Antigone Vocabulary Magic Squares 2 Answer Key

Match the definition with the vocabulary word. Put your answers in the magic squares below. When your answers are correct, all columns and rows will add to the same number.

A. BRAWL
B. CITADEL
C. CLEMENT
D. INSOLENCE
E. CONTEMPT
F. DIVINERS
G. GALES
H. SATED
I. AUSPICIOUS
J. BARROW
K. BRAY
L. TORMENTED
M. BLASPHEMY
N. CONSIDER
O. ENDURED
P. EMBERS

1. Inclined to be lenient or merciful
2. Large mound of earth or stones placed over a burial site
3. Those who can predict the future
4. Bore with tolerance
5. Small, glowing pieces of coal or wood, as in a dying fire
6. Feeling or attitude of regarding someone or something as inferior
7. Attended by favorable circumstances
8. Rudeness or disrespect
9. Profane act, utterance, or writing concerning God
10. Satisfied to excess
11. Caused great physical pain or mental anguish
12. Noisy quarrel or fight
13. Fortress in a commanding position in or near a city
14. Loud, harsh sound resembling that of a donkey
15. Very strong winds
16. Think carefully about

| A=12 | B=13 | C=1 | D=8 |
|---|---|---|---|
| E=6 | F=3 | G=15 | H=10 |
| I=7 | J=2 | K=14 | L=11 |
| M=9 | N=16 | O=4 | P=5 |

Antigone Vocabulary Magic Squares 3

Match the definition with the vocabulary word. Put your answers in the magic squares below. When your answers are correct, all columns and rows will add to the same number.

A. CARRION
B. SULTRY
C. COMPULSIVE
D. GALES
E. EDDY
F. CONSIDER
G. BARBARIC
H. EMBERS
I. TRANSCENDS
J. VIGIL
K. DEMORALIZING
L. PIETY
M. BRAZEN
N. SENTRIES
O. TRANSGRESS
P. LITHE

1. Commit an offense by violating a law or command; sin
2. Watch kept during normal sleeping hours
3. Small, glowing pieces of coal or wood, as in a dying fire
4. Feeding on dead and decaying flesh
5. Very strong winds
6. Current of water moving against the direction of the main current
7. Undermining the confidence or morale of; dishearten
8. Guards, especially soldiers posted at a given spot to prevent the passage of unauthorized persons
9. Think carefully about
10. Having the capacity to exert a strong, irresistible influence on
11. Made of brass
12. Quality of being pious or reverent
13. Passes beyond the limits of something
14. Marked by effortless grace
15. Very humid and hot
16. Without civilizing influences

| A= | B= | C= | D= |
|---|---|---|---|
| E= | F= | G= | H= |
| I= | J= | K= | L= |
| M= | N= | O= | P= |

Antigone Vocabulary Magic Squares 3 Answer Key

Match the definition with the vocabulary word. Put your answers in the magic squares below. When your answers are correct, all columns and rows will add to the same number.

A. CARRION
B. SULTRY
C. COMPULSIVE
D. GALES
E. EDDY
F. CONSIDER
G. BARBARIC
H. EMBERS
I. TRANSCENDS
J. VIGIL
K. DEMORALIZING
L. PIETY
M. BRAZEN
N. SENTRIES
O. TRANSGRESS
P. LITHE

1. Commit an offense by violating a law or command; sin
2. Watch kept during normal sleeping hours
3. Small, glowing pieces of coal or wood, as in a dying fire
4. Feeding on dead and decaying flesh
5. Very strong winds
6. Current of water moving against the direction of the main current
7. Undermining the confidence or morale of; dishearten
8. Guards, especially soldiers posted at a given spot to prevent the passage of unauthorized persons
9. Think carefully about
10. Having the capacity to exert a strong, irresistible influence on
11. Made of brass
12. Quality of being pious or reverent
13. Passes beyond the limits of something
14. Marked by effortless grace
15. Very humid and hot
16. Without civilizing influences

| A=4 | B=15 | C=10 | D=5 |
| --- | --- | --- | --- |
| E=6 | F=9 | G=16 | H=3 |
| I=13 | J=2 | K=7 | L=12 |
| M=11 | N=8 | O=1 | P=14 |

Antigone Vocabulary Magic Squares 4

Match the definition with the vocabulary word. Put your answers in the magic squares below. When your answers are correct, all columns and rows will add to the same number.

A. DEFY
B. DEFERENCE
C. SUBORDINATE
D. TRANSCENDS
E. AUGURY
F. CONTEMPT
G. CLEMENT
H. COMPREHENSIVE
I. DEFLECTS
J. LAMENTATION
K. ANARCHISTS
L. DROWSE
M. CALAMITY
N. DECREE
O. BLASPHEMY
P. BARROW

1. Event that brings terrible loss; disaster
2. Feeling or attitude of regarding someone or something as inferior
3. Marked by or showing extensive understanding
4. Profane act, utterance, or writing concerning God
5. To be half asleep
6. Subject to the authority or control of another
7. Refuse to submit to or cooperate with
8. Cry of sorrow and grief
9. Those who reject all forms of coercive control and authority
10. Passes beyond the limits of something
11. Yielding to the opinion, wishes, or judgment of another
12. Turns aside or causes to turn aside
13. Authoritative order having the force of law
14. Art, ability, or practice of making predictions
15. Inclined to be lenient or merciful
16. Large mound of earth or stones placed over a burial site

| A= | B= | C= | D= |
|---|---|---|---|
| E= | F= | G= | H= |
| I= | J= | K= | L= |
| M= | N= | O= | P= |

Antigone Vocabulary Magic Squares 4 Answer Key

Match the definition with the vocabulary word. Put your answers in the magic squares below. When your answers are correct, all columns and rows will add to the same number.

A. DEFY
B. DEFERENCE
C. SUBORDINATE
D. TRANSCENDS
E. AUGURY
F. CONTEMPT
G. CLEMENT
H. COMPREHENSIVE
I. DEFLECTS
J. LAMENTATION
K. ANARCHISTS
L. DROWSE
M. CALAMITY
N. DECREE
O. BLASPHEMY
P. BARROW

1. Event that brings terrible loss; disaster
2. Feeling or attitude of regarding someone or something as inferior
3. Marked by or showing extensive understanding
4. Profane act, utterance, or writing concerning God
5. To be half asleep
6. Subject to the authority or control of another
7. Refuse to submit to or cooperate with
8. Cry of sorrow and grief
9. Those who reject all forms of coercive control and authority
10. Passes beyond the limits of something
11. Yielding to the opinion, wishes, or judgment of another
12. Turns aside or causes to turn aside
13. Authoritative order having the force of law
14. Art, ability, or practice of making predictions
15. Inclined to be lenient or merciful
16. Large mound of earth or stones placed over a burial site

| A=7 | B=11 | C=6 | D=10 |
| --- | --- | --- | --- |
| E=14 | F=2 | G=15 | H=3 |
| I=12 | J=8 | K=9 | L=5 |
| M=1 | N=13 | O=4 | P=16 |

Antigone Vocabulary Juggle Letters 1

1. SUDOER = 1. _____
Excited, as to anger or action; stirred up

2. HSAPROMI = 2. _____
Tersely phrased statement of a truth or opinion; an adage

3. AETDS = 3. _____
Satisfied to excess

4. ROPW = 4. _____
Forward part of a ship's hull

5. PLMUECIVOS = 5. _____
Having the capacity to exert a strong, irresistible influence on

6. SMREEB = 6. _____
Small, glowing pieces of coal or wood, as in a dying fire

7. OSCRDIEN = 7. _____
Think carefully about

8. YRSLUT = 8. _____
Very humid and hot

9. ERTSSENI = 9. _____
Guards, especially soldiers posted at a given spot to prevent the passage of unauthorized persons

10. LOCENEINS =10. _____
Rudeness or disrespect

11. FEYD =11. _____
Refuse to submit to or cooperate with

12. LRIAPEV =12. _____
To be greater in strength or influence; triumph

13. DEYD =13. _____
Current of water moving against the direction of the main current

14. CTERHWDE =14. _____
In a deplorable state of distress or misfortune

Antigone Vocabulary Juggle Letters 1 Answer Key

1. SUDOER = 1. ROUSED
   Excited, as to anger or action; stirred up

2. HSAPROMI = 2. APHORISM
   Tersely phrased statement of a truth or opinion; an adage

3. AETDS = 3. SATED
   Satisfied to excess

4. ROPW = 4. PROW
   Forward part of a ship's hull

5. PLMUECIVOS = 5. COMPULSIVE
   Having the capacity to exert a strong, irresistible influence on

6. SMREEB = 6. EMBERS
   Small, glowing pieces of coal or wood, as in a dying fire

7. OSCRDIEN = 7. CONSIDER
   Think carefully about

8. YRSLUT = 8. SULTRY
   Very humid and hot

9. ERTSSENI = 9. SENTRIES
   Guards, especially soldiers posted at a given spot to prevent the passage of unauthorized persons

10. LOCENEINS = 10. INSOLENCE
    Rudeness or disrespect

11. FEYD = 11. DEFY
    Refuse to submit to or cooperate with

12. LRIAPEV = 12. PREVAIL
    To be greater in strength or influence; triumph

13. DEYD = 13. EDDY
    Current of water moving against the direction of the main current

14. CTERHWDE = 14. WRETCHED
    In a deplorable state of distress or misfortune

Antigone Vocabulary Juggle Letters 2

1. LAELBPAMIC = 1. _____
   Impossible to placate or appease

2. SRDUEO = 2. _____
   Excited, as to anger or action; stirred up

3. AIRBCABR = 3. _____
   Without civilizing influences

4. DYDE = 4. _____
   Current of water moving against the direction of the main current

5. SUIAOCPISU = 5. _____
   Attended by favorable circumstances

6. NEVGCENEA = 6. _____
   Infliction of punishment in return for a wrong committed

7. SRAYTA = 7. _____
   Away from the right or good; straying to or into wrong or evil ways

8. RNCTNSSDAE = 8. _____
   Passes beyond the limits of something

9. TYLSRU = 9. _____
   Very humid and hot

10. IAEMTLAONNT = 10. _____
    Cry of sorrow and grief

11. ROWP = 11. _____
    Forward part of a ship's hull

12. VNSMECIOPHEER = 12. _____
    Marked by or showing extensive understanding

13. MNDTROTEE = 13. _____
    Caused great physical pain or mental anguish

14. STRENSSAGR = 14. _____
    Commit an offense by violating a law or command; sin

Antigone Vocabulary Juggle Letters 2 Answer Key

1. LAELBPAMIC = 1. IMPLACABLE
   Impossible to placate or appease

2. SRDUEO = 2. ROUSED
   Excited, as to anger or action; stirred up

3. AIRBCABR = 3. BARBARIC
   Without civilizing influences

4. DYDE = 4. EDDY
   Current of water moving against the direction of the main current

5. SUIAOCPISU = 5. AUSPICIOUS
   Attended by favorable circumstances

6. NEVGCENEA = 6. VENGEANCE
   Infliction of punishment in return for a wrong committed

7. SRAYTA = 7. ASTRAY
   Away from the right or good; straying to or into wrong or evil ways

8. RNCTNSSDAE = 8. TRANSCENDS
   Passes beyond the limits of something

9. TYLSRU = 9. SULTRY
   Very humid and hot

10. IAEMTLAONNT = 10. LAMENTATION
    Cry of sorrow and grief

11. ROWP = 11. PROW
    Forward part of a ship's hull

12. VNSMECIOPHEER = 12. COMPREHENSIVE
    Marked by or showing extensive understanding

13. MNDTROTEE = 13. TORMENTED
    Caused great physical pain or mental anguish

14. STRENSSAGR = 14. TRANSGRESS
    Commit an offense by violating a law or command; sin

Antigone Vocabulary Juggle Letters 3

1. AORBWR = 1. _____
Large mound of earth or stones placed over a burial site

2. RWDOSE = 2. _____
To be half asleep

3. LSREANIT = 3. _____
Internal organs, especially the intestines

4. LOLYF = 4. _____
Lack of good sense, understanding, or foresight

5. ARYAST = 5. _____
Away from the right or good; straying to or into wrong or evil ways

6. USTYRL = 6. _____
Very humid and hot

7. CSSAUPIIUO = 7. _____
Attended by favorable circumstances

8. ENUREDD = 8. _____
Bore with tolerance

9. MATYLICA = 9. _____
Event that brings terrible loss; disaster

10. LGUT = 10. _____
Fill beyond capacity, especially with food

11. MHSYPABLE = 11. _____
Profane act, utterance, or writing concerning God

12. EEPERVSR = 12. _____
Obstinately persisting in an error or fault; wrongly self-willed or stubborn

13. GIEDRS = 13. _____
Funeral hymns

14. ETIYP = 14. _____
Quality of being pious or reverent

Antigone Vocabulary Juggle Letters 3 Answer Key

1. AORBWR = 1. BARROW
Large mound of earth or stones placed over a burial site

2. RWDOSE = 2. DROWSE
To be half asleep

3. LSREANIT = 3. ENTRAILS
Internal organs, especially the intestines

4. LOLYF = 4. FOLLY
Lack of good sense, understanding, or foresight

5. ARYAST = 5. ASTRAY
Away from the right or good; straying to or into wrong or evil ways

6. USTYRL = 6. SULTRY
Very humid and hot

7. CSSAUPIIUO = 7. AUSPICIOUS
Attended by favorable circumstances

8. ENUREDD = 8. ENDURED
Bore with tolerance

9. MATYLICA = 9. CALAMITY
Event that brings terrible loss; disaster

10. LGUT = 10. GLUT
Fill beyond capacity, especially with food

11. MHSYPABLE = 11. BLASPHEMY
Profane act, utterance, or writing concerning God

12. EEPERVSR = 12. PERVERSE
Obstinately persisting in an error or fault; wrongly self-willed or stubborn

13. GIEDRS = 13. DIRGES
Funeral hymns

14. ETIYP = 14. PIETY
Quality of being pious or reverent

Antigone Vocabulary Juggle Letters 4

1. RTSBDAINUEO = 1. _____
   Subject to the authority or control of another

2. ABWRRO = 2. _____
   Large mound of earth or stones placed over a burial site

3. AIDLZMNGRIOE = 3. _____
   Undermining the confidence or morale of; dishearten

4. PNSIROHEEEVCM = 4. _____
   Marked by or showing extensive understanding

5. SSNTRIEE = 5. _____
   Guards, especially soldiers posted at a given spot to prevent the passage of unauthorized persons

6. UTYRLS = 6. _____
   Very humid and hot

7. RABY = 7. _____
   Loud, harsh sound resembling that of a donkey

8. LSAGE = 8. _____
   Very strong winds

9. YDFE = 9. _____
   Refuse to submit to or cooperate with

10. RLWAB = 10. _____
    Noisy quarrel or fight

11. DDYE = 11. _____
    Current of water moving against the direction of the main current

12. LMRHSAA = 12. _____
    Military officer of the highest rank in some countries

13. REEFNCEED = 13. _____
    Yielding to the opinion, wishes, or judgment of another

14. IONMCRAAOPLT = 14. _____
    Official, formal, public announcement

Antigone Vocabulary Juggle Letters 4 Answer Key

1. RTSBDAINUEO = 1. SUBORDINATE
   Subject to the authority or control of another

2. ABWRRO = 2. BARROW
   Large mound of earth or stones placed over a burial site

3. AIDLZMNGRIOE = 3. DEMORALIZING
   Undermining the confidence or morale of; dishearten

4. PNSIROHEEEVCM = 4. COMPREHENSIVE
   Marked by or showing extensive understanding

5. SSNTRIEE = 5. SENTRIES
   Guards, especially soldiers posted at a given spot to prevent the passage of unauthorized persons

6. UTYRLS = 6. SULTRY
   Very humid and hot

7. RABY = 7. BRAY
   Loud, harsh sound resembling that of a donkey

8. LSAGE = 8. GALES
   Very strong winds

9. YDFE = 9. DEFY
   Refuse to submit to or cooperate with

10. RLWAB = 10. BRAWL
    Noisy quarrel or fight

11. DDYE = 11. EDDY
    Current of water moving against the direction of the main current

12. LMRHSAA = 12. MARSHAL
    Military officer of the highest rank in some countries

13. REEFNCEED = 13. DEFERENCE
    Yielding to the opinion, wishes, or judgment of another

14. IONMCRAAOPLT = 14. PROCLAMATION
    Official, formal, public announcement

Antigone Vocabulary Word Search 1

```
B A R R O W D M V G B K K F V V K Q P S S
W B A R B A R I C D B H P T O J S D X U J
P R E V A I L X V M V E R X S L L E V B X
B N E K C A L S W I E A N Q T A L F Q O B
G L U T D E F E R E N C E D I C T Y A R B
L A A H C L N T F S G E B N U A A E N D F
A H H S L H S C G Y E P R C T R J Z D I N
M S F X P R E R D Y A R F S T R E D D N G
E R X L E H E D T F N O V S J I A D C A Z
N A S B E S E E M C W A I S O V I A T K
T M M W S G I M T M E R R S L N Q V L E L
A E S T W P R C Y W O D I R G E S C A S A
T U Z W O D P O G I E R Q F E H I D M R U
I J G P R R D N S F E T A R R T B W I E S
O D Y U D X M T L U F L C A I S Q T V P
N E Z A R B Y E V S L E D D I L G N Y R I
D S H T H Y C M N I D T E Q J Z E R S E C
B U G F T T D P D T G L R S F M I E G P I
R O Y L S Q K T C N E I Z Y E T L N Z G O
T R A N S C E N D S S D L L A M J G F U
C O N S I D E R P S Y L C T G B R A W L S
```

Art, ability, or practice of making predictions (6)
Attended by favorable circumstances (10)
Authoritative order having the force of law (6)
Away from the right or good; straying to or into wrong or evil ways (6)
Bore with tolerance (7)
Caused great physical pain or mental anguish (9)
Commit an offense by violating a law or command; sin (10)
Cry of sorrow and grief (11)
Current of water moving against the direction of the main current (4)
Deserving of contempt or scorn (4)
Event that brings terrible loss; disaster (8)
Excited, as to anger or action; stirred up (6)
Feeding on dead and decaying flesh (7)
Feeling or attitude of regarding someone or something as inferior (8)
Fill beyond capacity, especially with food (4)
Formal command (5)
Fortress in a commanding position in or near a city (7)
Forward part of a ship's hull (4)
Funeral hymns (6)
Give up (an advantage, for example) to another; concede (5)
In a deplorable state of distress or misfortune (8)
Inclined to be lenient or merciful (7)
Infliction of punishment in return for a wrong committed (9)
Internal organs, especially the intestines (8)
Lack of good sense, understanding, or foresight (5)

Large mound of earth or stones placed over a burial site (6)
Loud, harsh sound resembling that of a donkey (4)
Made of brass (6)
Make or become less tense, taut, or firm; loosen (7)
Marked by effortless grace (5)
Military officer of the highest rank in some countries (7)
Noisy quarrel or fight (5)
Obstinately persisting in an error or fault; wrongly self-willed or stubborn (8)
Passes beyond the limits of something (10)
Profane act, utterance, or writing concerning God (9)
Quality of being pious or reverent (5)
Refuse to submit to or cooperate with (4)
Satisfied to excess (5)
Small, glowing pieces of coal or wood, as in a dying fire (6)
Subject to the authority or control of another (11)
Think carefully about (8)
Those who can predict the future (8)
To be greater in strength or influence; triumph (7)
To be half asleep (6)
Turns aside or causes to turn aside (8)
Undermining the confidence or morale of; dishearten (12)
Very humid and hot (6)
Very strong winds (5)
Watch kept during normal sleeping hours (5)
Without civilizing influences (8)
Yielding to the opinion, wishes, or judgment of another (9)

# Antigone Vocabulary Word Search 1 Answer Key

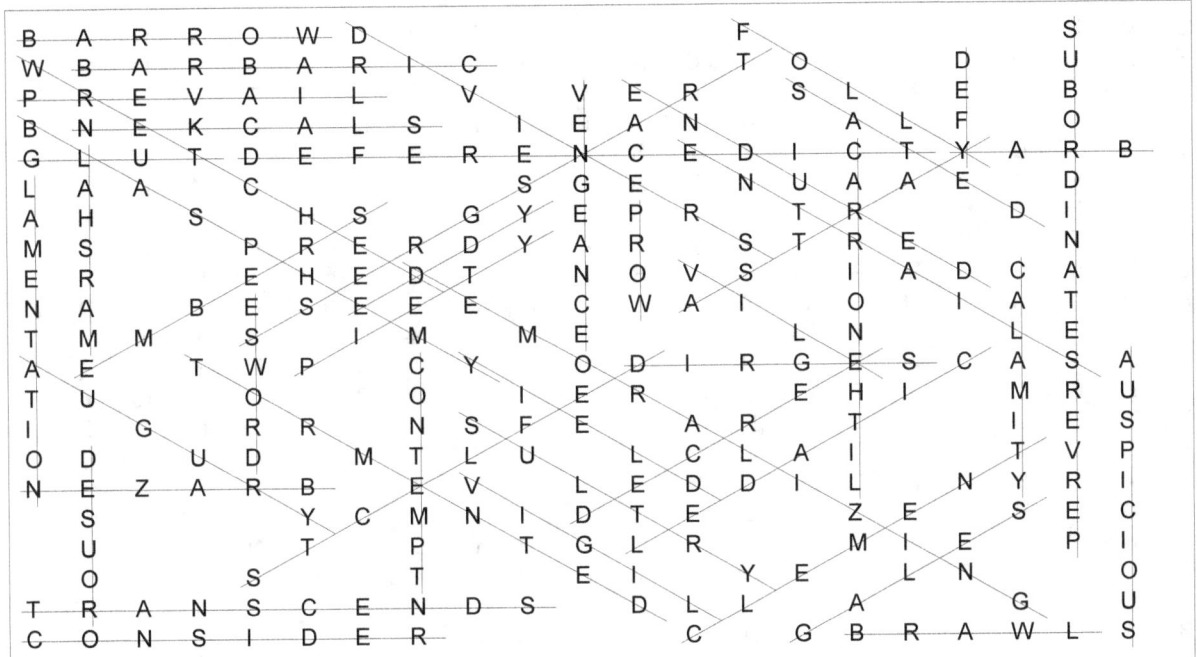

Art, ability, or practice of making predictions (6)
Attended by favorable circumstances (10)
Authoritative order having the force of law (6)
Away from the right or good; straying to or into wrong or evil ways (6)
Bore with tolerance (7)
Caused great physical pain or mental anguish (9)
Commit an offense by violating a law or command; sin (10)
Cry of sorrow and grief (11)
Current of water moving against the direction of the main current (4)
Deserving of contempt or scorn (4)
Event that brings terrible loss; disaster (8)
Excited, as to anger or action; stirred up (6)
Feeding on dead and decaying flesh (7)
Feeling or attitude of regarding someone or something as inferior (8)
Fill beyond capacity, especially with food (4)
Formal command (5)
Fortress in a commanding position in or near a city (7)
Forward part of a ship's hull (4)
Funeral hymns (6)
Give up (an advantage, for example) to another; concede (5)
In a deplorable state of distress or misfortune (8)
Inclined to be lenient or merciful (7)
Infliction of punishment in return for a wrong committed (9)
Internal organs, especially the intestines (8)
Lack of good sense, understanding, or foresight (5)

Large mound of earth or stones placed over a burial site (6)
Loud, harsh sound resembling that of a donkey (4)
Made of brass (6)
Make or become less tense, taut, or firm; loosen (7)
Marked by effortless grace (5)
Military officer of the highest rank in some countries (7)
Noisy quarrel or fight (5)
Obstinately persisting in an error or fault; wrongly self-willed or stubborn (8)
Passes beyond the limits of something (10)
Profane act, utterance, or writing concerning God (9)
Quality of being pious or reverent (5)
Refuse to submit to or cooperate with (4)
Satisfied to excess (5)
Small, glowing pieces of coal or wood, as in a dying fire (6)
Subject to the authority or control of another (11)
Think carefully about (8)
Those who can predict the future (8)
To be greater in strength or influence; triumph (7)
To be half asleep (6)
Turns aside or causes to turn aside (8)
Undermining the confidence or morale of; dishearten (12)
Very humid and hot (6)
Very strong winds (5)
Watch kept during normal sleeping hours (5)
Without civilizing influences (8)
Yielding to the opinion, wishes, or judgment of another (9)

Antigone Vocabulary Word Search 2

```
Z V H C B G L U T B Y C E D D Y D L B C D
E N D U R E D C R O A L R L R R E I A O K
P P T F K S I A A M R E Z T O T C T R M H
C R R S F D W Q N S T M C F W L R H R P N
G O W O E L I V S T S E E B S U E E O U Z
A W M Y U X H E C L A N D N E S E C W L G
L M H P B S R J E F A T N P T N L N F S W
E L R G R G E S N W Q C H Q E E E E O I C
S D M L S E A D D M R X K Z D H D L L V Y
P P C N Y U H L S B A E A E T G A O L E Q
G V A D G T B E C L J R T T N W T S Y N K
G R R U I X Y I N A B A S C Y C I N Y G S
T B R A Y R D Y L S S D V H H R C I T E Y
D Y I Y P Q G E R P I D E I A E Q X I A D
V S O V P H Q E F H Y V E F G L D R M N C
F T N B P R O S S E V S E F Y I T P A C G
V D I V I N E R S M R R J Z L N L B L E Q
T H N J E W H V I Y Q E M V E E W N A S Q
T P M E T N O C A S M B N S X B C F C S Y
M M Z V Y Y L F G I M M G C W F B T K J F
B A R B A R I C N M L E Z K E L H C S R G
```

Art, ability, or practice of making predictions (6)
Authoritative order having the force of law (6)
Away from the right or good; straying to or into wrong or evil ways (6)
Bore with tolerance (7)
Caused great physical pain or mental anguish (9)
Commit an offense by violating a law or command; sin (10)
Current of water moving against the direction of the main current (4)
Deserving of contempt or scorn (4)
Event that brings terrible loss; disaster (8)
Excited, as to anger or action; stirred up (6)
Feeding on dead and decaying flesh (7)
Feeling or attitude of regarding someone or something as inferior (8)
Fill beyond capacity, especially with food (4)
Formal command (5)
Fortress in a commanding position in or near a city (7)
Forward part of a ship's hull (4)
Funeral hymns (6)
Give up (an advantage, for example) to another; concede (5)
Guards, especially soldiers posted at a given spot to prevent the passage of unauthorized persons (8
Having the capacity to exert a strong, irresistible influence on (10)
In a deplorable state of distress or misfortune (8)
Inclined to be lenient or merciful (7)
Infliction of punishment in return for a wrong committed (9)

Lack of good sense, understanding, or foresight (5)
Large mound of earth or stones placed over a burial site (6)
Loud, harsh sound resembling that of a donkey (4)
Made of brass (6)
Make or become less tense, taut, or firm; loosen (7)
Marked by effortless grace (5)
Marked by or showing extensive understanding (13)
Military officer of the highest rank in some countries (7)
Noisy quarrel or fight (5)
Passes beyond the limits of something (10)
Profane act, utterance, or writing concerning God (9)
Quality of being pious or reverent (5)
Refuse to submit to or cooperate with (4)
Rudeness or disrespect (9)
Satisfied to excess (5)
Small, glowing pieces of coal or wood, as in a dying fire (6)
Tersely phrased statement of a truth or opinion; an adage (8)
Those who can predict the future (8)
To be greater in strength or influence; triumph (7)
To be half asleep (6)
Turns aside or causes to turn aside (8)
Very humid and hot (6)
Very strong winds (5)
Watch kept during normal sleeping hours (5)
Without civilizing influences (8)
Yielding to the opinion, wishes, or judgment of another (9)

# Antigone Vocabulary Word Search 2 Answer Key

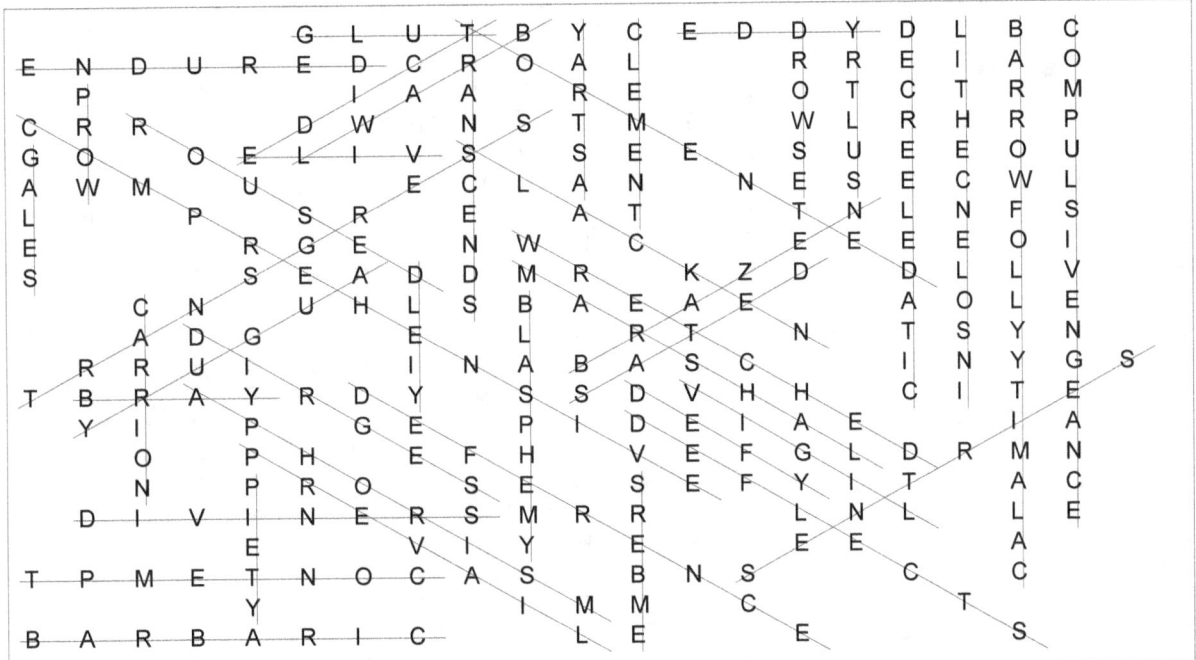

- Art, ability, or practice of making predictions (6)
- Authoritative order having the force of law (6)
- Away from the right or good; straying to or into wrong or evil ways (6)
- Bore with tolerance (7)
- Caused great physical pain or mental anguish (9)
- Commit an offense by violating a law or command; sin (10)
- Current of water moving against the direction of the main current (4)
- Deserving of contempt or scorn (4)
- Event that brings terrible loss; disaster (8)
- Excited, as to anger or action; stirred up (6)
- Feeding on dead and decaying flesh (7)
- Feeling or attitude of regarding someone or something as inferior (8)
- Fill beyond capacity, especially with food (4)
- Formal command (5)
- Fortress in a commanding position in or near a city (7)
- Forward part of a ship's hull (4)
- Funeral hymns (6)
- Give up (an advantage, for example) to another; concede (5)
- Guards, especially soldiers posted at a given spot to prevent the passage of unauthorized persons (8)
- Having the capacity to exert a strong, irresistible influence on (10)
- In a deplorable state of distress or misfortune (8)
- Inclined to be lenient or merciful (7)
- Infliction of punishment in return for a wrong committed (9)
- Lack of good sense, understanding, or foresight (5)
- Large mound of earth or stones placed over a burial site (6)
- Loud, harsh sound resembling that of a donkey (4)
- Made of brass (6)
- Make or become less tense, taut, or firm; loosen (7)
- Marked by effortless grace (5)
- Marked by or showing extensive understanding (13)
- Military officer of the highest rank in some countries (7)
- Noisy quarrel or fight (5)
- Passes beyond the limits of something (10)
- Profane act, utterance, or writing concerning God (9)
- Quality of being pious or reverent (5)
- Refuse to submit to or cooperate with (4)
- Rudeness or disrespect (9)
- Satisfied to excess (5)
- Small, glowing pieces of coal or wood, as in a dying fire (6)
- Tersely phrased statement of a truth or opinion; an adage (8)
- Those who can predict the future (8)
- To be greater in strength or influence; triumph (7)
- To be half asleep (6)
- Turns aside or causes to turn aside (8)
- Very humid and hot (6)
- Very strong winds (5)
- Watch kept during normal sleeping hours (5)
- Without civilizing influences (8)
- Yielding to the opinion, wishes, or judgment of another (9)

Antigone Vocabulary Word Search 3

```
T R A N S G R E S S A S T R A Y A G S B B
W G V C A E Y A S U L Z M L U D N L U A L
C P H G T M N C I L B G R S I A U B B A
F A P X E P T A G E T M G P R A T O B S
T F L H D E R R S U L R Y I G C V R A P
C O Q A H B T E R I A R K Y C E H E D H
A Z R T M N D E V H E N Y F I S I N I E
R I M E I V C S A V S R S O E S G N C M
R L B R T R E B I C O V U N T E A O Y
I C G H E N A Y D G G L U H S D S T M X
O P N P L M T P D N I C S L F U M N P G
N T I P Y R J E Y B L R E G T R L C X U E
T F Z F O L L Y D M R J D E P E P E G L N
T W I D C Y S M S N K S V F P D L V B S W
I R L L E K T X F Z P I R S M B S A D I S
N A A V D F C M R P S G B Y L R C J F V Q
S P R N L L E D J N W J S G E A D X G E S
O H O K S P L R E X R R C B L Z C C A W Y
L O M L V C F H E T E I M P X E O K L T M
E R E V I L E C O N T E M P T N E M E L C
N I D G L R D N I A C I D S S E N I S N K
C S J W P Y R V D H H E M I R N P P W D T
E M A M A H I E Y S E B D C C N Z R O E N
L R O R Q D L Q T P D E E B Y T N O R F G
B C B A R R O W R D R L E I Y Y W D Y H
```

| | | | | |
|---|---|---|---|---|
| ANARCHISTS | CARRION | DIRGES | INSOLENCE | SULTRY |
| APHORISM | CITADEL | DIVINERS | LITHE | TORMENTED |
| ASTRAY | CLEMENT | DROWSE | MARSHAL | TRANSCENDS |
| AUGURY | COMPREHENSIVE | EDDY | PERVERSE | TRANSGRESS |
| AUSPICIOUS | COMPULSIVE | EDICT | PIETY | VENGEANCE |
| BARBARIC | CONSIDER | EMBERS | PREVAIL | VIGIL |
| BARROW | CONTEMPT | ENDURED | PROW | VILE |
| BLASPHEMY | DECREE | ENTRAILS | ROUSED | WRETCHED |
| BRAWL | DEFERENCE | FOLLY | SATED | YIELD |
| BRAY | DEFLECTS | GALES | SENTRIES | |
| BRAZEN | DEFY | GLUT | SLACKEN | |
| CALAMITY | DEMORALIZING | IMPLACABLE | SUBORDINATE | |

Antigone Vocabulary Word Search 3 Answer Key

| ANARCHISTS | CARRION | DIRGES | INSOLENCE | SULTRY |
| APHORISM | CITADEL | DIVINERS | LITHE | TORMENTED |
| ASTRAY | CLEMENT | DROWSE | MARSHAL | TRANSCENDS |
| AUGURY | COMPREHENSIVE | EDDY | PERVERSE | TRANSGRESS |
| AUSPICIOUS | COMPULSIVE | EDICT | PIETY | VENGEANCE |
| BARBARIC | CONSIDER | EMBERS | PREVAIL | VIGIL |
| BARROW | CONTEMPT | ENDURED | PROW | VILE |
| BLASPHEMY | DECREE | ENTRAILS | ROUSED | WRETCHED |
| BRAWL | DEFERENCE | FOLLY | SATED | YIELD |
| BRAY | DEFLECTS | GALES | SENTRIES | |
| BRAZEN | DEFY | GLUT | SLACKEN | |
| CALAMITY | DEMORALIZING | IMPLACABLE | SUBORDINATE | |

## Antigone Vocabulary Word Search 4

```
A U S P I C I O U S U L T R Y C F H R V T
Y C P P R O C L A M A T I O N O W Y V R R
M O T N K Q X Z A M B Y B T K L M W J K A
K N C L K H Z D Y T T Y S P Y P B V M G N
Q T E S E N T R I E S D E W L R C V D C S
F E L S Q R Y M L Z G L W S E Z G F Z Z G
D M F C Q S A Q Z E W Q R T H D D F D R R
E P E C T L Z S C B X Y A E S E G R O E
C T D C A N G S M Z V L C T I N E S A O S
R Y N A Y R N Z K E A I A C H S B U L W S
E D I C Y R D I S N O C P E R V I M O E S D
L N V K A A R C V H G E L H C M R S E E
R B P U B S S R O A G N M D A E K L T C M
N R T R L A F K N T A I H N B A N N C N O
F W H P U M D Q M L X E B J A C E L Y E R
L P A P V I G I L G D A K M D I E L A
L O M S H I J V F P N Z E R E D T I O L
C Y C M L O L E W I L E N O F B Y H D S I
P R L W N G R S T W N V T E D L A E Y N Z
R G V A I L I S Y Y E R N E Z A R B I I
O K M K M V X E S A J E D F S U A K N
W G E C V H G T R M N H A S Y G R P L C G
F L N J K R U T P C M T D S U R F O L L Y
H H T T I L S Z E N I Z V A O T M V T P M
    G D G A N W X C G Y S W Q P V B P D K
```

| ANARCHISTS | CITADEL | DIVINERS | LITHE | TORMENTED |
| APHORISM | CLEMENT | DROWSE | MARSHAL | TRANSCENDS |
| ASTRAY | COMPREHENSIVE | EDDY | PERVERSE | TRANSGRESS |
| AUGURY | COMPULSIVE | EDICT | PIETY | VENGEANCE |
| AUSPICIOUS | CONSIDER | EMBERS | PREVAIL | VIGIL |
| BARBARIC | CONTEMPT | ENDURED | PROCLAMATION | VILE |
| BARROW | DECREE | ENTRAILS | PROW | WRETCHED |
| BRAWL | DEFERENCE | FOLLY | ROUSED | YIELD |
| BRAY | DEFLECTS | GALES | SATED | |
| BRAZEN | DEFY | GLUT | SENTRIES | |
| CALAMITY | DEMORALIZING | IMPLACABLE | SLACKEN | |
| CARRION | DIRGES | INSOLENCE | SULTRY | |

Antigone Vocabulary Word Search 4 Answer Key

| ANARCHISTS | CITADEL | DIVINERS | LITHE | TORMENTED |
| APHORISM | CLEMENT | DROWSE | MARSHAL | TRANSCENDS |
| ASTRAY | COMPREHENSIVE | EDDY | PERVERSE | TRANSGRESS |
| AUGURY | COMPULSIVE | EDICT | PIETY | VENGEANCE |
| AUSPICIOUS | CONSIDER | EMBERS | PREVAIL | VIGIL |
| BARBARIC | CONTEMPT | ENDURED | PROCLAMATION | VILE |
| BARROW | DECREE | ENTRAILS | PROW | WRETCHED |
| BRAWL | DEFERENCE | FOLLY | ROUSED | YIELD |
| BRAY | DEFLECTS | GALES | SATED | |
| BRAZEN | DEFY | GLUT | SENTRIES | |
| CALAMITY | DEMORALIZING | IMPLACABLE | SLACKEN | |
| CARRION | DIRGES | INSOLENCE | SULTRY | |

# Antigone Vocabulary Crossword 1

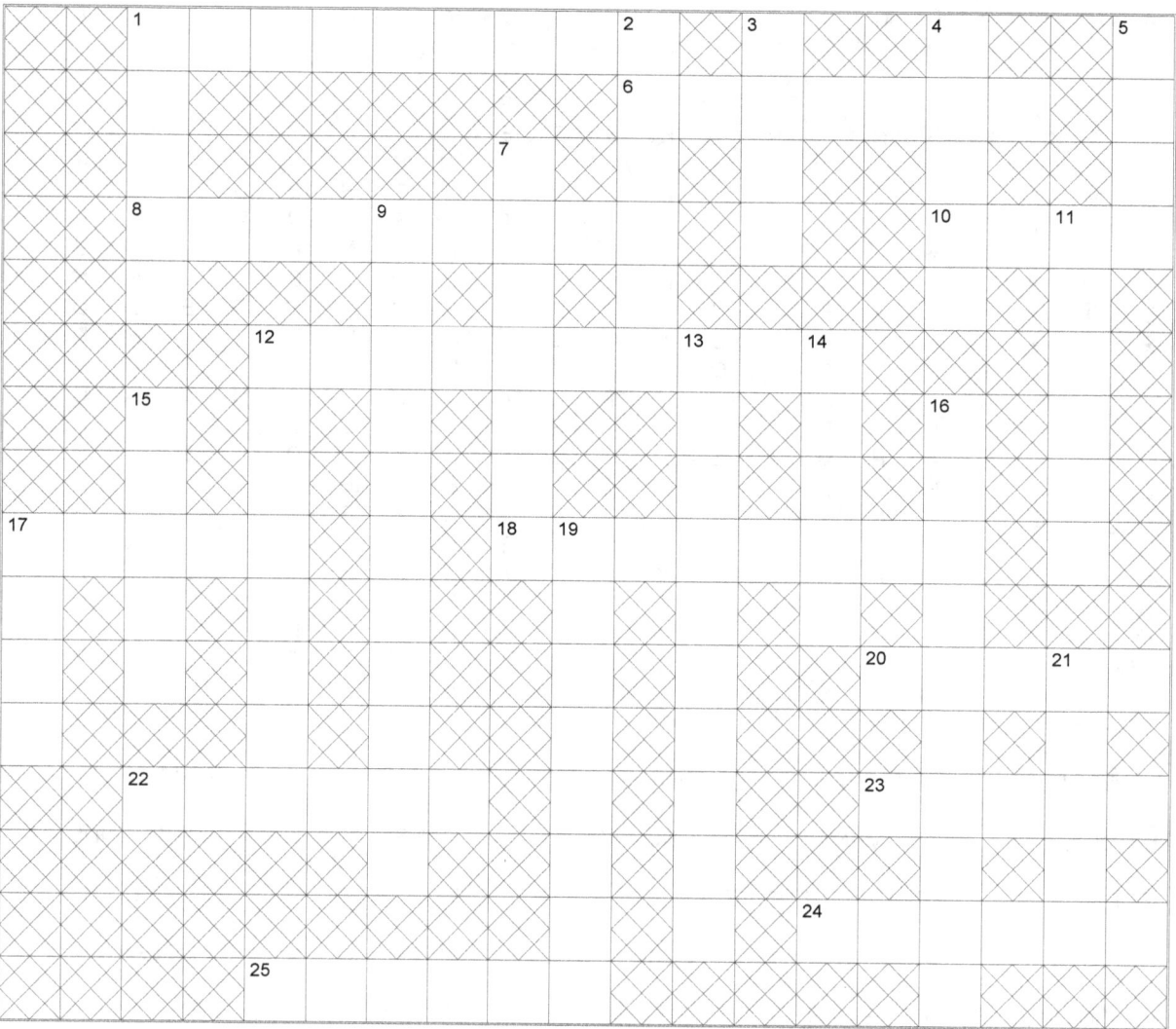

**Across**
1. Infliction of punishment in return for a wrong committed
6. Military officer of the highest rank in some countries
8. Rudeness or disrespect
10. Current of water moving against the direction of the main current
12. Having the capacity to exert a strong, irresistible influence on
17. Very strong winds
18. Turns aside or causes to turn aside
20. Give up (an advantage, for example) to another; concede
22. Large mound of earth or stones placed over a burial site
23. Quality of being pious or reverent
24. Excited, as to anger or action; stirred up
25. Funeral hymns

**Down**
1. Watch kept during normal sleeping hours
2. Small, glowing pieces of coal or wood, as in a dying fire
3. Loud, harsh sound resembling that of a donkey
4. Satisfied to excess
5. Refuse to submit to or cooperate with
7. Bore with tolerance
9. Cry of sorrow and grief
11. To be half asleep
12. Think carefully about
13. Impossible to placate or appease
14. Formal command
15. Lack of good sense, understanding, or foresight
16. Attended by favorable circumstances
17. Fill beyond capacity, especially with food
19. Internal organs, especially the intestines
21. Marked by effortless grace

# Antigone Vocabulary Crossword 1 Answer Key

|   | 1  |   |   |   |   |   | 2 |   | 3 |   | 4 |   | 5 |
|---|----|---|---|---|---|---|---|---|---|---|---|---|---|
|   | V  | E | N | G | E | A | N | C | E |   | S |   | D |
|   | I  |   |   |   |   |   | 6 M | A | R | S | H | A | L | E |
|   | G  |   |   |   | 7 E |   | B |   | A |   | T |   | F |
|   | 8 I | N | S | 9 O | L | E | N | C | E |   | 10 E | 11 D | Y |
|   | L  |   |   | A |   | D |   | R |   |   | D |   | R |
|   |    |   | 12 C | O | M | P | U | L | 13 S | 14 I | V | E |   |   | O |
|   | 15 F |   | O | E |   | R |   |   | M |   | D |   | 16 A |   | W |
|   | O  |   | N | N |   | E |   |   | P |   | I |   | U |   | S |
| 17 G | A | L | E | S | T |   | 18 D | 19 E | F | L | E | C | T | S |   | E |
| L |   | L |   | I |   | A |   | N |   | A |   | T |   | P |
| U |   | Y |   | D |   | T |   | T |   | C |   |   | 20 Y | I | E | L | 21 D |
| T |   |   |   | E |   | I |   | R |   | A |   |   | C |   | I |
|   | 22 B | A | R | R | O | W |   | A |   | B |   | 23 P | I | E | T | Y |
|   |    |   |   | N |   |   |   | I |   | L |   | O |   | H |
|   |    |   |   |   |   |   |   | L |   | E |   | 24 R | O | U | S | E | D |
|   |    |   | 25 D | I | R | G | E | S |   |   |   | S |

Across
1. Infliction of punishment in return for a wrong committed
6. Military officer of the highest rank in some countries
8. Rudeness or disrespect
10. Current of water moving against the direction of the main current
12. Having the capacity to exert a strong, irresistible influence on
17. Very strong winds
18. Turns aside or causes to turn aside
20. Give up (an advantage, for example) to another; concede
22. Large mound of earth or stones placed over a burial site
23. Quality of being pious or reverent
24. Excited, as to anger or action; stirred up
25. Funeral hymns

Down
1. Watch kept during normal sleeping hours
2. Small, glowing pieces of coal or wood, as in a dying fire
3. Loud, harsh sound resembling that of a donkey
4. Satisfied to excess
5. Refuse to submit to or cooperate with
7. Bore with tolerance
9. Cry of sorrow and grief
11. To be half asleep
12. Think carefully about
13. Impossible to placate or appease
14. Formal command
15. Lack of good sense, understanding, or foresight
16. Attended by favorable circumstances
17. Fill beyond capacity, especially with food
19. Internal organs, especially the intestines
21. Marked by effortless grace

# Antigone Vocabulary Crossword 2

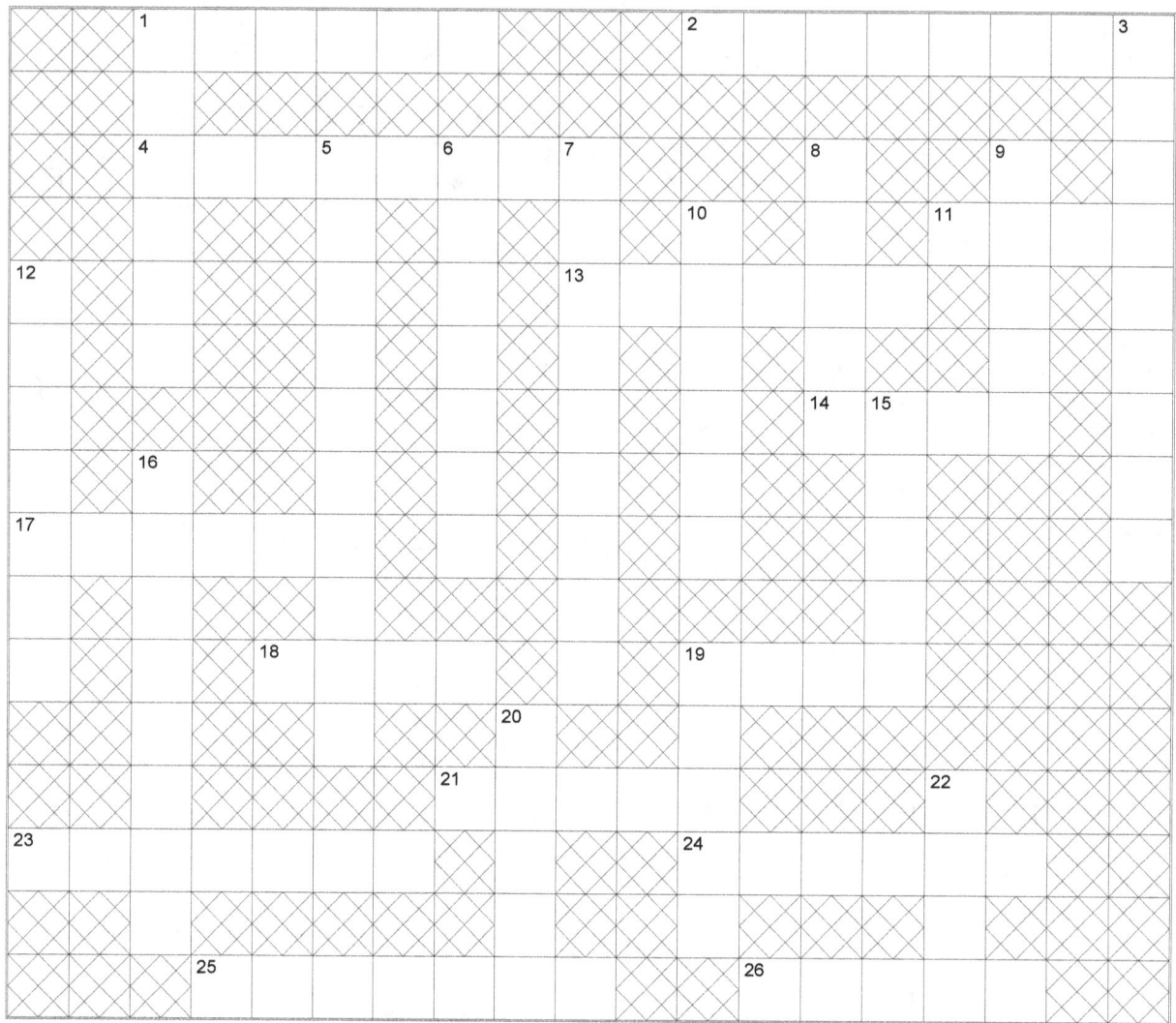

**Across**
1. Funeral hymns
2. In a deplorable state of distress or misfortune
4. Feeling or attitude of regarding someone or something as inferior
11. Deserving of contempt or scorn
13. Excited, as to anger or action; stirred up
14. Refuse to submit to or cooperate with
17. To be half asleep
18. Current of water moving against the direction of the main current
19. Fill beyond capacity, especially with food
21. Watch kept during normal sleeping hours
23. Inclined to be lenient or merciful
24. Small, glowing pieces of coal or wood, as in a dying fire
25. Make or become less tense, taut, or firm; loosen
26. Noisy quarrel or fight

**Down**
1. Authoritative order having the force of law
3. Yielding to the opinion, wishes, or judgment of another
5. Passes beyond the limits of something
6. Military officer of the highest rank in some countries
7. Caused great physical pain or mental anguish
8. Give up (an advantage, for example) to another; concede
9. Quality of being pious or reverent
10. Very humid and hot
12. Fortress in a commanding position in or near a city
15. Formal command
16. Think carefully about
19. Very strong winds
20. Marked by effortless grace
22. Forward part of a ship's hull

# Antigone Vocabulary Crossword 2 Answer Key

|   | 1 D | I | R | G | E | S |   |   | 2 W | R | E | T | C | H | E | 3 D |
|---|---|---|---|---|---|---|---|---|---|---|---|---|---|---|---|---|
|   | E |   |   |   |   |   |   |   |   |   |   |   |   |   |   | E |
|   | 4 C | O | 5 N | T | 6 E | M | 7 P | T |   | 8 Y |   |   | 9 P |   | F |
|   | R |   | R |   | A |   | O |   | 10 S | I |   | 11 V | I | L | E |
| 12 C | E |   | A |   | R |   | 13 R | O | U | S | E | D |   | E |   | R |
| I | E |   | N |   | S |   | M |   | L |   |   | L |   | T |   | E |
| T |   |   | S |   | H |   | E |   | T |   | 14 D | 15 E | F | Y |   | N |
| A |   | 16 C |   | C |   | A |   | N |   | R |   | D |   |   |   | C |
| 17 D | R | O | W | S | E |   | L |   | T |   | Y |   | I |   |   | E |
| E |   | N |   | N |   |   |   |   | E |   |   |   | C |   |   |   |
| L |   | S |   | 18 E | D | D | Y |   | D |   | 19 G | L | U | T |   |   |
|   |   | I |   |   | S |   | 20 L |   |   |   | A |   |   |   |   |   |
|   |   | 21 D |   |   | V | I | G | I | L |   |   |   |   | 22 P |   |   |
| 23 C | L | E | M | E | N | T |   | T |   |   | 24 E | M | B | E | R | S |
|   |   | R |   |   |   |   |   | H |   |   | S |   |   | O |   |   |
|   |   |   | 25 S | L | A | C | K | E | N |   | 26 B | R | A | W | L |   |

**Across**
1. Funeral hymns
2. In a deplorable state of distress or misfortune
4. Feeling or attitude of regarding someone or something as inferior
11. Deserving of contempt or scorn
13. Excited, as to anger or action; stirred up
14. Refuse to submit to or cooperate with
17. To be half asleep
18. Current of water moving against the direction of the main current
19. Fill beyond capacity, especially with food
21. Watch kept during normal sleeping hours
23. Inclined to be lenient or merciful
24. Small, glowing pieces of coal or wood, as in a dying fire
25. Make or become less tense, taut, or firm; loosen
26. Noisy quarrel or fight

**Down**
1. Authoritative order having the force of law
3. Yielding to the opinion, wishes, or judgment of another
5. Passes beyond the limits of something
6. Military officer of the highest rank in some countries
7. Caused great physical pain or mental anguish
8. Give up (an advantage, for example) to another; concede
9. Quality of being pious or reverent
10. Very humid and hot
12. Fortress in a commanding position in or near a city
15. Formal command
16. Think carefully about
19. Very strong winds
20. Marked by effortless grace
22. Forward part of a ship's hull

# Antigone Vocabulary Crossword 3

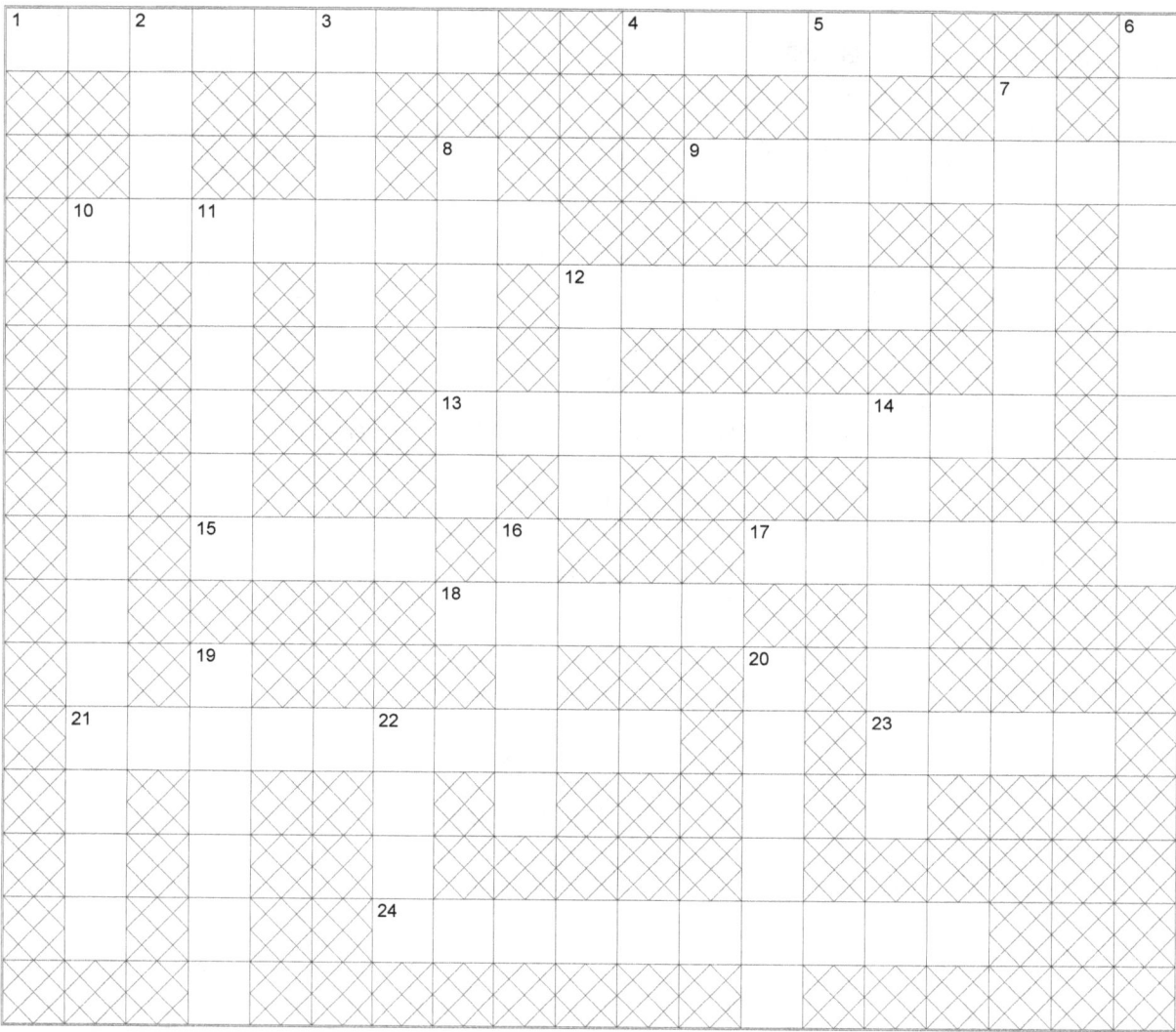

**Across**
1. Those who can predict the future
4. Give up (an advantage, for example) to another; concede
9. Internal organs, especially the intestines
10. Obstinately persisting in an error or fault; wrongly self-willed or stubborn
12. Made of brass
13. Those who reject all forms of coercive control and authority
15. Refuse to submit to or cooperate with
17. Noisy quarrel or fight
18. Satisfied to excess
21. Commit an offense by violating a law or command; sin
23. Current of water moving against the direction of the main current
24. Passes beyond the limits of something

**Down**
2. Deserving of contempt or scorn
3. Small, glowing pieces of coal or wood, as in a dying fire
5. Marked by effortless grace
6. Rudeness or disrespect
7. Funeral hymns
8. Away from the right or good; straying to or into wrong or evil ways
10. Official, formal, public announcement
11. Excited, as to anger or action; stirred up
12. Loud, harsh sound resembling that of a donkey
14. Make or become less tense, taut, or firm; loosen
16. Very strong winds
19. Large mound of earth or stones placed over a burial site
20. Authoritative order having the force of law
22. Fill beyond capacity, especially with food

Antigone Vocabulary Crossword 3 Answer Key

**Across**
1. Those who can predict the future
4. Give up (an advantage, for example) to another; concede
9. Internal organs, especially the intestines
10. Obstinately persisting in an error or fault; wrongly self-willed or stubborn
12. Made of brass
13. Those who reject all forms of coercive control and authority
15. Refuse to submit to or cooperate with
17. Noisy quarrel or fight
18. Satisfied to excess
21. Commit an offense by violating a law or command; sin
23. Current of water moving against the direction of the main current
24. Passes beyond the limits of something

**Down**
2. Deserving of contempt or scorn
3. Small, glowing pieces of coal or wood, as in a dying fire
5. Marked by effortless grace
6. Rudeness or disrespect
7. Funeral hymns
8. Away from the right or good; straying to or into wrong or evil ways
10. Official, formal, public announcement
11. Excited, as to anger or action; stirred up
12. Loud, harsh sound resembling that of a donkey
14. Make or become less tense, taut, or firm; loosen
16. Very strong winds
19. Large mound of earth or stones placed over a burial site
20. Authoritative order having the force of law
22. Fill beyond capacity, especially with food

# Antigone Vocabulary Crossword 4

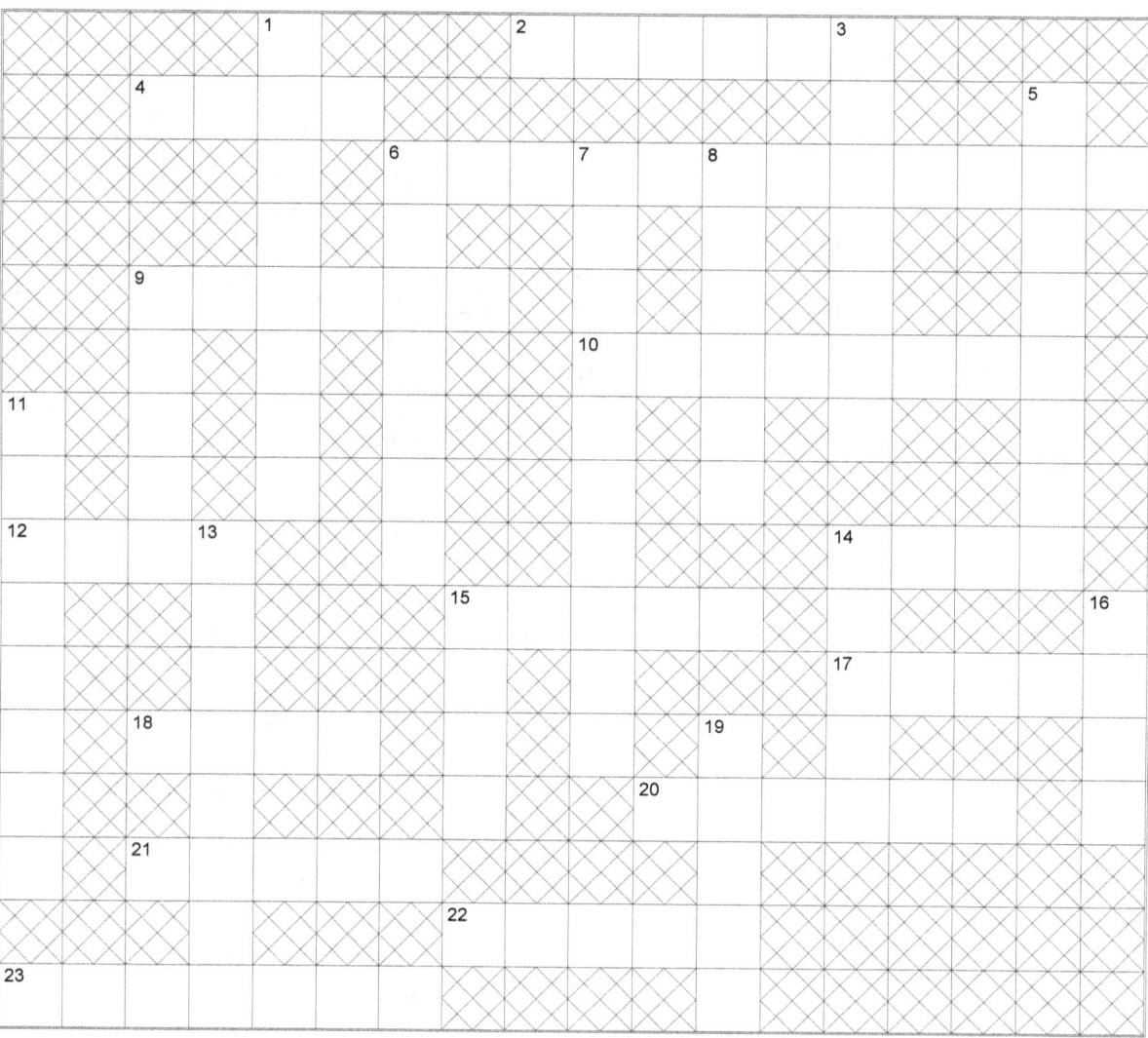

**Across**

2. Small, glowing pieces of coal or wood, as in a dying fire
4. Loud, harsh sound resembling that of a donkey
6. Official, formal, public announcement
9. Made of brass
10. Obstinately persisting in an error or fault; wrongly self-willed or stubborn
12. Deserving of contempt or scorn
14. Fill beyond capacity, especially with food
15. Formal command
17. Marked by effortless grace
18. Forward part of a ship's hull
20. Excited, as to anger or action; stirred up
21. Give up (an advantage, for example) to another; concede
22. Watch kept during normal sleeping hours
23. Military officer of the highest rank in some countries

**Down**

1. Without civilizing influences
3. Make or become less tense, taut, or firm; loosen
5. Feeling or attitude of regarding someone or something as inferior
6. To be greater in strength or influence; triumph
7. Having the capacity to exert a strong, irresistible influence on
8. Away from the right or good; straying to or into wrong or evil ways
9. Noisy quarrel or fight
11. Those who can predict the future
13. Internal organs, especially the intestines
14. Very strong winds
15. Current of water moving against the direction of the main current
16. Refuse to submit to or cooperate with
19. Lack of good sense, understanding, or foresight

## Antigone Vocabulary Crossword 4 Answer Key

|   |   |   |   | ¹B |   |   | ²E | M | B | E | R | ³S |   |   |   |
|---|---|---|---|---|---|---|---|---|---|---|---|---|---|---|---|
|   |   | ⁴B | R | A | Y |   |   |   |   |   |   | L |   | ⁵C |   |
|   |   |   |   | R |   | ⁶P | R | O | ⁷C | L | ⁸A | M | A | T | I | O | N |
|   |   |   |   | B |   | R |   |   | O |   | S |   |   | C |   | N |
|   |   | ⁹B | R | A | Z | E | N |   | M |   | T |   | ⁸K |   |   | T |
|   |   | R |   | R |   | V |   | ¹⁰P | E | R | V | E | R | S | E |
| ¹¹D |   | A |   | I |   | A |   | U |   |   | A |   | N |   | M |
| I |   | W |   | C |   | I |   | L |   |   | Y |   |   |   | P |
| ¹²V | I | ¹³L | E |   |   | L |   | S |   |   | ¹⁴G | L | U | T |   | ¹⁶D |
| I |   | N |   |   | ¹⁵E | D | I | C | T |   | A |   |   |   | D |
| N |   | T |   |   |   | D |   | V |   |   | ¹⁷L | I | T | H | E |
| E |   | ¹⁸P | R | O | W |   | D |   | ¹⁹F |   | E |   |   |   | F |
| R |   | A |   |   |   |   | Y |   | ²⁰R | O | U | S | E | D |   | Y |
| S |   | ²¹Y | I | E | L | D |   |   | L |   |   |   |   |   |
|   |   | L |   |   |   | ²²V | I | G | I | L |   |   |   |   |
| ²³M | A | R | S | H | A | L |   |   | Y |   |   |   |   |   |

Across
2. Small, glowing pieces of coal or wood, as in a dying fire
4. Loud, harsh sound resembling that of a donkey
6. Official, formal, public announcement
9. Made of brass
10. Obstinately persisting in an error or fault; wrongly self-willed or stubborn
12. Deserving of contempt or scorn
14. Fill beyond capacity, especially with food
15. Formal command
17. Marked by effortless grace
18. Forward part of a ship's hull
20. Excited, as to anger or action; stirred up
21. Give up (an advantage, for example) to another; concede
22. Watch kept during normal sleeping hours
23. Military officer of the highest rank in some countries

Down
1. Without civilizing influences
3. Make or become less tense, taut, or firm; loosen
5. Feeling or attitude of regarding someone or something as inferior
6. To be greater in strength or influence; triumph
7. Having the capacity to exert a strong, irresistible influence on
8. Away from the right or good; straying to or into wrong or evil ways
9. Noisy quarrel or fight
11. Those who can predict the future
13. Internal organs, especially the intestines
14. Very strong winds
15. Current of water moving against the direction of the main current
16. Refuse to submit to or cooperate with
19. Lack of good sense, understanding, or foresight

| | |
|---|---|
| ANARCHISTS | Those who reject all forms of coercive control and authority |
| APHORISM | Tersely phrased statement of a truth or opinion; an adage |
| ASTRAY | Away from the right or good; straying to or into wrong or evil ways |
| AUGURY | Art, ability, or practice of making predictions |
| AUSPICIOUS | Attended by favorable circumstances |

| | |
|---|---|
| BARBARIC | Without civilizing influences |
| BARROW | Large mound of earth or stones placed over a burial site |
| BLASPHEMY | Profane act, utterance, or writing concerning God |
| BRAWL | Noisy quarrel or fight |
| BRAY | Loud, harsh sound resembling that of a donkey |

| BRAZEN | Made of brass |
|---|---|
| CALAMITY | Event that brings terrible loss; disaster |
| CARRION | Feeding on dead and decaying flesh |
| CITADEL | Fortress in a commanding position in or near a city |
| CLEMENT | Inclined to be lenient or merciful |

| | |
|---|---|
| COMPREHENSIVE | Marked by or showing extensive understanding |
| COMPULSIVE | Having the capacity to exert a strong, irresistible influence on |
| CONSIDER | Think carefully about |
| CONTEMPT | Feeling or attitude of regarding someone or something as inferior |
| DECREE | Authoritative order having the force of law |

| | |
|---|---|
| DEFERENCE | Yielding to the opinion, wishes, or judgment of another |
| DEFLECTS | Turns aside or causes to turn aside |
| DEFY | Refuse to submit to or cooperate with |
| DEMORALIZING | Undermining the confidence or morale of; dishearten |
| DIRGES | Funeral hymns |

| | |
|---|---|
| DIVINERS | Those who can predict the future |
| DROWSE | To be half asleep |
| EDDY | Current of water moving against the direction of the main current |
| EDICT | Formal command |
| EMBERS | Small, glowing pieces of coal or wood, as in a dying fire |

| | |
|---|---|
| ENDURED | Bore with tolerance |
| ENTRAILS | Internal organs, especially the intestines |
| FOLLY | Lack of good sense, understanding, or foresight |
| GALES | Very strong winds |
| GLUT | Fill beyond capacity, especially with food |

| | |
|---|---|
| IMPLACABLE | Impossible to placate or appease |
| INSOLENCE | Rudeness or disrespect |
| LAMENTATION | Cry of sorrow and grief |
| LITHE | Marked by effortless grace |
| MARSHAL | Military officer of the highest rank in some countries |

| | |
|---|---|
| PERVERSE | Obstinately persisting in an error or fault; wrongly self-willed or stubborn |
| PIETY | Quality of being pious or reverent |
| PREVAIL | To be greater in strength or influence; triumph |
| PROCLAMATION | Official, formal, public announcement |
| PROW | Forward part of a ship's hull |

| | |
|---|---|
| ROUSED | Excited, as to anger or action; stirred up |
| SATED | Satisfied to excess |
| SENTRIES | Guards, especially soldiers posted at a given spot to prevent the passage of unauthorized persons |
| SLACKEN | Make or become less tense, taut, or firm; loosen |
| SUBORDINATE | Subject to the authority or control of another |

| SULTRY | Very humid and hot |
| --- | --- |
| TORMENTED | Caused great physical pain or mental anguish |
| TRANSCENDS | Passes beyond the limits of something |
| TRANSGRESS | Commit an offense by violating a law or command; sin |
| VENGEANCE | Infliction of punishment in return for a wrong committed |

| | |
|---|---|
| VIGIL | Watch kept during normal sleeping hours |
| VILE | Deserving of contempt or scorn |
| WRETCHED | In a deplorable state of distress or misfortune |
| YIELD | Give up (an advantage, for example) to another; concede |

## Antigone Vocabulary

| SULTRY | BRAZEN | ASTRAY | PIETY | LITHE |
|---|---|---|---|---|
| DIVINERS | BRAWL | DEFLECTS | MARSHAL | EDDY |
| COMPREHENSIVE | CARRION | FREE SPACE | DEFERENCE | BRAY |
| SLACKEN | IMPLACABLE | AUGURY | DEMORALIZING | ENDURED |
| PROCLAMATION | TORMENTED | SATED | PERVERSE | CALAMITY |

## Antigone Vocabulary

| EMBERS | TRANSCENDS | BARBARIC | GALES | FOLLY |
|---|---|---|---|---|
| GLUT | CONTEMPT | DROWSE | CITADEL | VENGEANCE |
| WRETCHED | VILE | FREE SPACE | TRANSGRESS | BLASPHEMY |
| APHORISM | CLEMENT | ROUSED | DIRGES | INSOLENCE |
| PREVAIL | DECREE | EDICT | ENTRAILS | COMPULSIVE |

## Antigone Vocabulary

| VENGEANCE | ENTRAILS | GLUT | CALAMITY | SLACKEN |
|---|---|---|---|---|
| LITHE | CLEMENT | DEFY | APHORISM | CONSIDER |
| ENDURED | BRAY | FREE SPACE | EMBERS | LAMENTATION |
| DEFLECTS | ASTRAY | SUBORDINATE | DEFERENCE | PROCLAMATION |
| DEMORALIZING | TRANSGRESS | GALES | FOLLY | DIVINERS |

## Antigone Vocabulary

| AUSPICIOUS | PERVERSE | YIELD | TRANSCENDS | IMPLACABLE |
|---|---|---|---|---|
| PREVAIL | CARRION | TORMENTED | BARROW | VIGIL |
| CONTEMPT | MARSHAL | FREE SPACE | SENTRIES | WRETCHED |
| BARBARIC | EDDY | AUGURY | VILE | COMPREHENSIVE |
| PROW | COMPULSIVE | DIRGES | BRAWL | SATED |

## Antigone Vocabulary

| COMPREHENSIVE | BARROW | CITADEL | WRETCHED | DEFERENCE |
|---|---|---|---|---|
| DIRGES | VIGIL | TRANSCENDS | SLACKEN | FOLLY |
| PROW | PROCLAMATION | FREE SPACE | ENTRAILS | SULTRY |
| VILE | SUBORDINATE | LITHE | ASTRAY | CALAMITY |
| BRAZEN | ROUSED | BARBARIC | INSOLENCE | TRANSGRESS |

## Antigone Vocabulary

| IMPLACABLE | COMPULSIVE | DIVINERS | ANARCHISTS | DROWSE |
|---|---|---|---|---|
| BRAY | TORMENTED | EDICT | CONSIDER | DEFLECTS |
| DEFY | BRAWL | FREE SPACE | YIELD | GLUT |
| BLASPHEMY | APHORISM | SENTRIES | AUSPICIOUS | DEMORALIZING |
| GALES | SATED | VENGEANCE | CONTEMPT | DECREE |

## Antigone Vocabulary

| BLASPHEMY | AUGURY | SATED | BARROW | PROW |
|---|---|---|---|---|
| VIGIL | CONSIDER | IMPLACABLE | ASTRAY | LAMENTATION |
| GALES | BARBARIC | FREE SPACE | BRAWL | DECREE |
| CLEMENT | CARRION | ROUSED | CONTEMPT | VENGEANCE |
| DEMORALIZING | MARSHAL | EDDY | PIETY | CALAMITY |

## Antigone Vocabulary

| CITADEL | COMPULSIVE | AUSPICIOUS | YIELD | PERVERSE |
|---|---|---|---|---|
| PROCLAMATION | SENTRIES | BRAY | COMPREHENSIVE | GLUT |
| LITHE | DROWSE | FREE SPACE | FOLLY | DEFERENCE |
| VILE | DEFLECTS | ANARCHISTS | WRETCHED | DIRGES |
| ENTRAILS | SULTRY | TRANSCENDS | ENDURED | TORMENTED |

Antigone Vocabulary

| ENTRAILS | PIETY | SLACKEN | MARSHAL | DIVINERS |
|---|---|---|---|---|
| DIRGES | LITHE | EDICT | PERVERSE | TRANSCENDS |
| VILE | DROWSE | FREE SPACE | DEMORALIZING | SUBORDINATE |
| VIGIL | ROUSED | CITADEL | CONTEMPT | COMPREHENSIVE |
| YIELD | PROCLAMATION | CALAMITY | BRAY | SULTRY |

Antigone Vocabulary

| TRANSGRESS | DEFY | FOLLY | COMPULSIVE | BARROW |
|---|---|---|---|---|
| VENGEANCE | SENTRIES | BRAWL | GLUT | CLEMENT |
| APHORISM | GALES | FREE SPACE | ASTRAY | INSOLENCE |
| PREVAIL | DEFLECTS | DEFERENCE | PROW | LAMENTATION |
| IMPLACABLE | DECREE | AUGURY | ENDURED | CONSIDER |

## Antigone Vocabulary

| | | | | |
|---|---|---|---|---|
| AUSPICIOUS | DECREE | CITADEL | COMPULSIVE | DIVINERS |
| CLEMENT | WRETCHED | VENGEANCE | ENDURED | PROCLAMATION |
| BRAY | YIELD | FREE SPACE | VILE | SLACKEN |
| PIETY | DIRGES | LITHE | BARROW | SULTRY |
| AUGURY | APHORISM | TORMENTED | ASTRAY | LAMENTATION |

## Antigone Vocabulary

| | | | | |
|---|---|---|---|---|
| DEFLECTS | PREVAIL | GLUT | DEFERENCE | VIGIL |
| CARRION | INSOLENCE | EDDY | IMPLACABLE | DEFY |
| MARSHAL | DROWSE | FREE SPACE | BLASPHEMY | FOLLY |
| BARBARIC | TRANSGRESS | TRANSCENDS | PERVERSE | BRAWL |
| SUBORDINATE | ANARCHISTS | CONSIDER | ROUSED | EMBERS |

## Antigone Vocabulary

| AUGURY | PIETY | EDICT | EDDY | BARBARIC |
|---|---|---|---|---|
| ENDURED | TORMENTED | CONSIDER | WRETCHED | IMPLACABLE |
| SULTRY | CARRION | FREE SPACE | TRANSCENDS | CONTEMPT |
| SATED | PROW | LITHE | ENTRAILS | CLEMENT |
| DEFERENCE | PERVERSE | SLACKEN | VILE | BRAY |

## Antigone Vocabulary

| YIELD | GLUT | ASTRAY | ANARCHISTS | VIGIL |
|---|---|---|---|---|
| SUBORDINATE | TRANSGRESS | BRAWL | SENTRIES | DROWSE |
| ROUSED | INSOLENCE | FREE SPACE | AUSPICIOUS | DIRGES |
| VENGEANCE | DEFY | PROCLAMATION | PREVAIL | CALAMITY |
| BARROW | DEMORALIZING | LAMENTATION | FOLLY | COMPULSIVE |

## Antigone Vocabulary

| CONTEMPT | DIRGES | WRETCHED | DECREE | CITADEL |
|---|---|---|---|---|
| LITHE | DEFLECTS | APHORISM | GALES | AUSPICIOUS |
| DROWSE | SENTRIES | FREE SPACE | TRANSGRESS | DIVINERS |
| FOLLY | COMPREHENSIVE | BRAZEN | TRANSCENDS | CARRION |
| MARSHAL | SULTRY | LAMENTATION | YIELD | BARROW |

## Antigone Vocabulary

| BARBARIC | ENDURED | AUGURY | ASTRAY | CLEMENT |
|---|---|---|---|---|
| PERVERSE | EMBERS | VENGEANCE | BLASPHEMY | PROW |
| TORMENTED | BRAWL | FREE SPACE | PREVAIL | VIGIL |
| DEFERENCE | ROUSED | ENTRAILS | SLACKEN | DEMORALIZING |
| GLUT | INSOLENCE | VILE | IMPLACABLE | CALAMITY |

Antigone Vocabulary

| PERVERSE | CONSIDER | MARSHAL | LITHE | SULTRY |
|---|---|---|---|---|
| VILE | AUSPICIOUS | DEFLECTS | FOLLY | AUGURY |
| DIRGES | BRAZEN | FREE SPACE | TRANSCENDS | DEMORALIZING |
| BRAWL | EDICT | SATED | PIETY | DIVINERS |
| BLASPHEMY | COMPULSIVE | BARROW | PREVAIL | DEFERENCE |

Antigone Vocabulary

| DEFY | LAMENTATION | VENGEANCE | BARBARIC | TRANSGRESS |
|---|---|---|---|---|
| ASTRAY | CARRION | CITADEL | SUBORDINATE | CLEMENT |
| CONTEMPT | YIELD | FREE SPACE | TORMENTED | VIGIL |
| GLUT | SENTRIES | DECREE | ROUSED | INSOLENCE |
| GALES | PROW | BRAY | APHORISM | WRETCHED |

## Antigone Vocabulary

| CALAMITY | CONSIDER | DEFY | FOLLY | IMPLACABLE |
|---|---|---|---|---|
| APHORISM | ENDURED | LAMENTATION | EDDY | CARRION |
| VIGIL | BARBARIC | FREE SPACE | TRANSGRESS | SLACKEN |
| ROUSED | WRETCHED | DEMORALIZING | MARSHAL | CONTEMPT |
| CLEMENT | COMPREHENSIVE | SENTRIES | ANARCHISTS | GLUT |

## Antigone Vocabulary

| LITHE | TORMENTED | INSOLENCE | ENTRAILS | PROCLAMATION |
|---|---|---|---|---|
| SATED | EDICT | AUSPICIOUS | DEFERENCE | DIRGES |
| BRAWL | VILE | FREE SPACE | SULTRY | DECREE |
| TRANSCENDS | AUGURY | DEFLECTS | SUBORDINATE | ASTRAY |
| BRAY | BARROW | GALES | VENGEANCE | DIVINERS |

## Antigone Vocabulary

| CLEMENT | BARBARIC | CONSIDER | ANARCHISTS | GALES |
|---|---|---|---|---|
| EDICT | IMPLACABLE | MARSHAL | BLASPHEMY | SLACKEN |
| PREVAIL | SUBORDINATE | FREE SPACE | SULTRY | VIGIL |
| PIETY | DECREE | PROCLAMATION | LAMENTATION | COMPULSIVE |
| DIVINERS | EMBERS | EDDY | YIELD | AUGURY |

## Antigone Vocabulary

| DEFY | VILE | CONTEMPT | FOLLY | CARRION |
|---|---|---|---|---|
| INSOLENCE | GLUT | APHORISM | ASTRAY | CITADEL |
| ROUSED | BARROW | FREE SPACE | DROWSE | TRANSGRESS |
| SENTRIES | PROW | CALAMITY | TRANSCENDS | VENGEANCE |
| WRETCHED | DEFLECTS | ENDURED | SATED | PERVERSE |

## Antigone Vocabulary

| EDDY | FOLLY | CITADEL | BARROW | CONSIDER |
|---|---|---|---|---|
| TRANSCENDS | LITHE | DIRGES | PERVERSE | BRAWL |
| LAMENTATION | SATED | FREE SPACE | BRAY | GALES |
| DEFY | ANARCHISTS | TRANSGRESS | PREVAIL | CLEMENT |
| VENGEANCE | EMBERS | ASTRAY | DEFERENCE | INSOLENCE |

## Antigone Vocabulary

| YIELD | COMPREHENSIVE | AUSPICIOUS | CONTEMPT | SLACKEN |
|---|---|---|---|---|
| ENTRAILS | CALAMITY | PIETY | DIVINERS | IMPLACABLE |
| COMPULSIVE | SULTRY | FREE SPACE | AUGURY | DEFLECTS |
| BLASPHEMY | CARRION | WRETCHED | MARSHAL | APHORISM |
| EDICT | PROW | VIGIL | ENDURED | PROCLAMATION |

## Antigone Vocabulary

| YIELD | ENTRAILS | PROW | BRAY | MARSHAL |
|---|---|---|---|---|
| ANARCHISTS | WRETCHED | EDDY | DECREE | LITHE |
| INSOLENCE | CONTEMPT | FREE SPACE | VIGIL | AUGURY |
| PERVERSE | PREVAIL | ROUSED | SENTRIES | CLEMENT |
| BRAWL | SULTRY | SLACKEN | ASTRAY | PIETY |

## Antigone Vocabulary

| DEMORALIZING | AUSPICIOUS | BLASPHEMY | CARRION | DEFERENCE |
|---|---|---|---|---|
| BARBARIC | ENDURED | TRANSGRESS | COMPULSIVE | BARROW |
| APHORISM | PROCLAMATION | FREE SPACE | FOLLY | EDICT |
| GLUT | VENGEANCE | DEFY | COMPREHENSIVE | EMBERS |
| DROWSE | IMPLACABLE | DIRGES | TRANSCENDS | VILE |

## Antigone Vocabulary

| COMPULSIVE | YIELD | TRANSCENDS | AUSPICIOUS | PIETY |
|---|---|---|---|---|
| DECREE | CALAMITY | IMPLACABLE | GLUT | BARROW |
| LITHE | DEFLECTS | FREE SPACE | CONSIDER | EDICT |
| VENGEANCE | FOLLY | BRAWL | VIGIL | DEMORALIZING |
| ENTRAILS | AUGURY | EDDY | PERVERSE | ASTRAY |

## Antigone Vocabulary

| BLASPHEMY | SULTRY | PROCLAMATION | INSOLENCE | VILE |
|---|---|---|---|---|
| WRETCHED | ENDURED | CARRION | SLACKEN | CITADEL |
| BRAZEN | MARSHAL | FREE SPACE | PROW | TORMENTED |
| DEFERENCE | SENTRIES | ANARCHISTS | SUBORDINATE | GALES |
| CONTEMPT | COMPREHENSIVE | LAMENTATION | TRANSGRESS | BRAY |

Antigone Vocabulary

| IMPLACABLE | VENGEANCE | ROUSED | MARSHAL | CARRION |
|---|---|---|---|---|
| TRANSCENDS | PERVERSE | PREVAIL | PIETY | COMPREHENSIVE |
| DEMORALIZING | BARROW | FREE SPACE | LAMENTATION | CONSIDER |
| DEFERENCE | PROW | VILE | LITHE | CITADEL |
| DIRGES | GALES | YIELD | EMBERS | WRETCHED |

Antigone Vocabulary

| GLUT | EDDY | DECREE | DEFY | AUGURY |
|---|---|---|---|---|
| FOLLY | ENDURED | PROCLAMATION | AUSPICIOUS | ANARCHISTS |
| ENTRAILS | CONTEMPT | FREE SPACE | DROWSE | SENTRIES |
| APHORISM | BRAWL | COMPULSIVE | CLEMENT | TORMENTED |
| EDICT | ASTRAY | SLACKEN | DEFLECTS | BLASPHEMY |

## Antigone Vocabulary

| VIGIL | CARRION | DEFLECTS | BLASPHEMY | BRAWL |
|---|---|---|---|---|
| BRAY | TORMENTED | YIELD | TRANSCENDS | COMPULSIVE |
| LAMENTATION | PREVAIL | FREE SPACE | WRETCHED | DEFY |
| PERVERSE | SUBORDINATE | VILE | BARROW | FOLLY |
| APHORISM | BARBARIC | ROUSED | EMBERS | EDICT |

## Antigone Vocabulary

| CALAMITY | TRANSGRESS | CLEMENT | PROW | COMPREHENSIVE |
|---|---|---|---|---|
| DIRGES | SULTRY | SATED | CONTEMPT | GLUT |
| DEMORALIZING | AUSPICIOUS | FREE SPACE | ENDURED | ASTRAY |
| PIETY | PROCLAMATION | BRAZEN | SENTRIES | INSOLENCE |
| DEFERENCE | DECREE | MARSHAL | AUGURY | EDDY |

www.ingramcontent.com/pod-product-compliance
Lightning Source LLC
Chambersburg PA
CBHW081453070526
44586CB00019B/2335